'The Southern around London'

The R C Riley Archive 1937 - 1964: Vol 4

Compiled by Jeremy Clarke

ISBN 978-1-913251-11-6

First Published in 2020 by Transport Treasury Publishing Ltd. 16 Highworth Close, High Wycombe, HP13 7PJ

www.ttpublishing.co.uk

Printed in the UK by Henry Ling Limited, at the Dorset Press, Dorchester. DT1 1HD.

Front cover: On Saturday 8th May 1954 "Battle of Britain" class pacific No 34087, *145 Squadron*, comes charging into Herne Hill, a brief 'Level' interlude in the 2¾-mile long climb, mainly at 1 in 101½, from Brixton to Penge tunnel. It is heading the 11.35am Victoria-Ramsgate express, first stop Bromley South. If this were a weekday the 11.35 would be the all-Pullman 'Kentish Belle', fast to Whitstable, allowed 80 minutes over those difficult fifty-nine miles of the former LCDR main line to the North Kent Coast. No 34087 came into traffic in December 1948, one of twenty engines built at Brighton Works to Order No 3383; rebuilding took place exactly twelve years later. At the time Dick took this photograph the engine was allocated to Ramsgate so is clearly 'working home'. One of the last survivors, *145 Squadron* was withdrawn from Eastleigh in July 1967. *RCR 5100*

Contents

Title page: The crew of Billinton 'E4' class 0-6-2T No 32468 have spotted something of interest during a brief lull in their carriage shunting duties at Clapham Junction. Loose shunting of passenger vehicles was restricted to very few places by the time Dick Riley took this photograph on 7th July 1950, Clapham Junction, with its yard of more than forty sidings, being one of them. The redoubtable Driver Bert Hooker considered these engines, with their powerful Westinghouse air brakes, ideal for this work. But then he may have been prejudiced, having begun his railway career at the ex-LBSCR shed at New Cross Gate where just about anything that moved was so fitted. The engine is attached to a shunting truck made from the frame of an old Beattie tender and has acquired an Ashford close-fitting smokebox door. Unusually, No 32468 bears no evidence of ownership. One of the earliest of its class, it left Brighton Works as No 468 in May 1898 bearing the name *Midhurst* and clothed in Stroudley's goods green livery, the Brighton paintshop presumably having concluded that any six-coupled engine must be for freight work. New Cross [Gate] based for most of its pre-Nationalisation career, the engine moved to Brighton after this short period at Nine Elms and was withdrawn from there in January 1963. *RCR 4054*

Opposite: On 31st July 1954 'N' class 2-6-0 No 31402 brings its train of vans spinning downgrade from Orpington to pass under this splendid ex-SER signal gantry at Chislehurst. The left-hand arm signals trains from the down Main line to the spur to St Mary Cray Junction on the ex-LCDR line to Chatham, while the middle signal indicates a movement from down Main to down Slow. The gantry lasted until signalling was renewed in conjunction with the Kent Coast Electrification Scheme when colour-lights controlled from the new Chislehurst Junction power box rendered it redundant from 31st May 1959. The engine, built at Ashford in August 1932 and one of the last of the class of eighty, enjoyed a life of thirty-two years, almost all based at Ashford, before withdrawal from Brighton shed in August 1963. *RCR 5204*

Rear cover: Norwood Junction shed opened in 1935 to reduce the mileage of engines travelling 'light' from New Cross Gate or West Croydon to shunt the extensive goods yards south of the station. Against the estimated cost of £33,125 were set savings put at roundly £2,000 pa. The dead-end shed tucked comfortably into the encircling arm of the Bromley Junction-Norwood Junction spur line, had five roads with a raised coal stage and a 65' turntable. When photographed on 3rd August 1959 the allocation consisted of three Billinton 'radial' tanks, four 'W' class 2-6-4T, eight 'C2x' and two 'Q' class 0-6-0s and nine diesel shunters. Among the latter was No 15201, one of three built at Ashford in 1937, all allocated new to 75C. Norwood closed in June 1964 and its site was cleared shortly afterwards before re-establishment as a contractors' maintenance depot. *RCR 14042*

Introduction

Searching out a representative selection of photographs under this title has to be straightforward, doesn't it? After all, Dick Riley produced a plethora of excellent images around the Capital over the years, particularly post-World War Two. But wait! How do you define 'London'? Nowadays it seems the M25 is often categorised as the limit though it runs almost entirely through the 'Green Belt'. Using that definition would certainly offend those who live inside that boundary but neither in a London Borough nor possessing a London postcode and who thus, in Southern territory anyway, defend their right to be addressed as living in Kent or Surrey. So, use the London telephone area '02' code perhaps? Ah, but then, particularly, Bromley's Petts Wood and Orpington (01689) and areas along the southern perimeter of Croydon (01737) will be lost.

The Southern never defined its 'London' traffic as such, not publicly anyway; in general its services were simply termed 'Suburban' or 'Main Line'. Yet 'Suburban' applied to trains going as far out as, say, Guildford, a thirty-mile journey from Waterloo, and Maidstone, forty miles beyond Victoria and even further from Charing Cross.

In defining London for my purpose, it seemed to me after much contemplation the most sensible approach was to take the limits set by the Freedom Pass I am fortunate to carry with me courtesy of my Local Authority. At least then the limit is unmistakably marked even if I can use the pass freely on Transport for London bus routes that poke out beyond it here and there – Bluewater, Westerham, Redhill, Dorking, Staines and Heathrow for example. The rather angular semi-circle I thus set myself follows a line from Dartford through Swanley, Knockholt, Upper Warlingham, Coulsdon South, the two Ewells, and Hampton to Feltham. You may not agree with this perhaps too restricted an approach and I admit there was a strong temptation to go further. But there have to be limits and I concluded this 'Limited London' provides in all respects a wealth of possibilities. I therefore make no apologies for this decision.

Dick Riley, a banker by profession, was himself a South Londoner, brought up in Tulse Hill, hence perhaps his deep interest in and wealth of knowledge about the 'Brighton'. Much of his adult life was spent in Beckenham; he commuted to the Capital from Shortlands. It ought not then to astonish that a substantial proportion of his 'Southern Around London' photos feature parts of the unlovely surroundings of Peckham and Brixton, grimy diversions to the sheds at Norwood Junction, New Cross Gate and Hither Green and the rather more salubrious areas about the ex-London, Chatham & Dover Railway main line between Herne Hill and Bickley. The eastern end of this provided a bonus with the former South Eastern Railway line bridging the Chatham one at Chislehurst Junction, the spurs between the two adding to the variety of traffic to be seen. However, Dick's tastes were wide-ranging and not limited to 'British Railways' though it is evident his admiration for the Great Western and its Western successor certainly matched if not exceeded that for the Southern.

From quite early on Dick clearly became acquainted with a range of railway staff, not just those 'on the ground' but with officialdom too that enabled him to gain passes to the lineside and for shed visits. The occasional footplate pass was also forthcoming and it is evident he was sometimes 'tipped off' about some particularly interesting or unusual event.

The predominance of static images in the older sections of the Transport Treasury lists leads me to conclude Dick's earlier camera(s) did not possess sufficient shutter speed for him to catch fast-moving trains with pinpoint sharpness. Indeed, almost all those from that period that do depict trains in motion have a slight degree of fuzziness about them. Nevertheless, those prints selected from this period are no less worthy of reproduction, telling a story especially of a late-1930s railway landscape irrevocably changed by the Second World War. Unfortunately, in many cases locations in these early lists are not noted so those of interest I felt I could not identify with precision sadly had to be put aside.

I wrote at the beginning of this Introduction that I

had a plethora of excellent images to choose from. I soon found out the hard way that for every picture picked I agonised over the need to discard three or four, perhaps more, equally attractive or informative ones. Research followed of course, to build on the minimal information Dick provided with almost all his photos, the pleasures and frustrations of finding and cross-checking various sources, quite often to back up or confirm an educated guess based on prior knowledge. But it has been a very interesting and satisfying search and I trust you will also find much of interest in my selection.

Finally, last but by no means least, my thanks to Mike King and Michael Blakemore for answered questions.

Jeremy Clarke, London, 2020.

The London, Chatham & Dover Railway's line running north from Herne Hill, eventually to reach the Metropolitan Railway at Farringdon, was the first to breach the City of London's boundaries. The railway bridge over Ludgate Hill was roundly condemned as obstructing the view of St Paul's from Ludgate Circus even if the Company offered some compensation by mounting a City 'shield' upon its faces. But the bridge carrying the line over the Thames, completed in 1864, was unashamedly advertised as LCDR property by two sets of the company's Coat of Arms, cast in iron and brightly coloured and mounted on each side at the south end of the structure. Dick Riley photographed the upstream one in rather sad post-war condition on 1st June 1951; it was restored to full glory c1990. ***RCR 4343***

1 Early Days

The finances of the London, Chatham & Dover Railway were never far from failure, a fact reflected in the simplicity of both its motive power and rolling stock. Yet Longhedge Works built up a tradition of excellent design and robust construction in its engines, making them easy on maintenance and ensuring high mileages between overhauls. And it is notable that after the company came to a working arrangement with the South Eastern in 1899 the influence of Longhedge predominated. In view of the financial problems it was perhaps inevitable that delivery of William Kirtley's ten 'T' class 0-6-0 shunting tank engines was over a period of no less than fourteen years, 1879-93. They were numbered 141-150 but after the fusion in 1899 had 459 added to become Nos 600-609. Following the 'A' for Ashford prefix to the numbers added by the Southern after grouping, 1000 was added instead from 1931 as shown here on number 1604. Works No 16, it came into service from Longhedge in 1891 and was one of only three of the class still at work at the outbreak of the Second World War. Whether any would have survived for much longer had that not occurred is doubtful. But all three came to BR in 1948. No 1604, pictured here at Stewarts Lane on 27th March 1937, was withdrawn from the former SER Reading South shed in November 1950. There appears to be some doubt over whether it ever carried the additional and allocated BR 30000. ***RCR 3***

Above: Dick Riley later became a regular visitor to Hither Green shed but captured this image of 'O1' class 0-6-0 No 1374 on 17th July 1937. Delivered by Sharp, Stewart in September 1891 as part of an order for ten 'O' class engines numbered 369-78 (Works Nos 3711-20), No 374 was one of fifty-nine members of the 122-strong class rebuilt by Wainwright with a domed boiler and larger cab and classified 'O1', in this case in August 1905. No 1374 was withdrawn in September 1949 and though the British Railways 30000 may have been allocated the engine never carried it. Stephenson Clarke – 'SC' on the wagon on the ramp – was among the companies contracted to supply the Southern with loco coal as it had been to both the LBSCR and SECR. ***RCR 17***

Right: The 'D1' class 0-4-2T typified William Stroudley's reign at Brighton, a neat, simple, yet aesthetically pleasing design exemplified by No 255, photographed at New Cross Gate shed in January 1939. As it still carries the 'B' prefix to the number - to identify it as an ex-LBSCR engine - rather than the '2000' addition introduced from 1931, the former ***Willingdon*** **must have been a long time out of the paintshop though the engineman appears to be happy with it. No 255 came into service in November 1881, one of the thirty-five examples built by Neilsons of Glasgow. To a class total of one hundred and twenty-five the engines could be seen throughout the Brighton system on all but the fastest and heaviest express passenger services. Apart from New Cross, concentration in London in LBSCR days was at Battersea with a few at West Croydon. No 255 was withdrawn in 1947.** ***RCR 313***

Left: 'U1' class 2-6-0 No 1908 is seen leaving Victoria in July 1937 with a train for Ramsgate, though the headcode makes no distinction between use of the main line through Herne Hill or the Catford Loop to reach Shortlands. The rectangular 'disc' on the top lamp iron with an evident 'reporting number' would imply this is an extra working. The engine was one of the last three of the class to be constructed, leaving Eastleigh Works in October 1931 and destined for Stewarts Lane. Post-war it spent time at Tonbridge before a final move to Norwood Junction following completion of the second phase of the Kent Coast Electrification in 1962. Its sojourn there was short, for it was one of seventeen members of the class swept aside at the end of that year. *RCR 16*

Opposite bottom: Messrs Beyer Peacock of Manchester provided many engines to the LSWR but William Adams turned to Neilsons of Glasgow for his main line freight power. No 395, the first of seventy 0-6-0s, arrived at Nine Elms in November 1881. They were powerful for their size and weight, the reason why fifty of them were commandeered by the Government during the First World War for service in the Middle East: none returned. Almost all had been 'duplicated' at the beginning of the 20th century, noted by a '0' in the books but a short bar below the number on the cabside. The Southern suppressed the bar and instead prefixed the number with an 'E' – for ex-LSWR engines - and the '0'. Things changed again with the addition of 3000 to the base number but the eighteen that came to BR were renumbered 30564-81 though not in date order. No 3496, (Neilsons Works No 3376), photographed at Feltham in company with Adams 'T1' class 0-4-4T No 9, probably in 1939, was into traffic in October 1885. The first in the batch of a modified design with slightly longer frames and therefore a ton heavier than the originals, it later acquired a Drummond chimney as shown here though retaining the Adams sloping front smokebox. Withdrawal as No 30579 came in January 1958. *RCR 343*

Above: The thirty engines of Drummond's '700' class were built by Dubs of Glasgow between March and June 1897 (Works Nos 3510-39), No 355 being one of the last. As the class was numbered in odd blocks, the first engine being No 687, the use of '700' for its class identification is something of a puzzle. No less so is the exact derivation of the name 'Black Motors' by which the engines came to be known as that colour was not unique to them. Altogether heavier and more powerful than Adams' '0395' class they were allocated to the major depots around the system to handle main line freight traffic. All thirty were later equipped with a superheater in a higher-pitched boiler, an extended smokebox and a stovepipe chimney. The process began under Urie's superintendency and was continued by the SR, this engine receiving the treatment in July 1929. Photographed at Clapham Junction, probably in 1939, No 355 acquired BR's additional 30000 after Nationalisation while allocated to Salisbury shed, and was the third member of the class to be withdrawn, in February 1961. *RCR 348*

SOUTHERN
2478

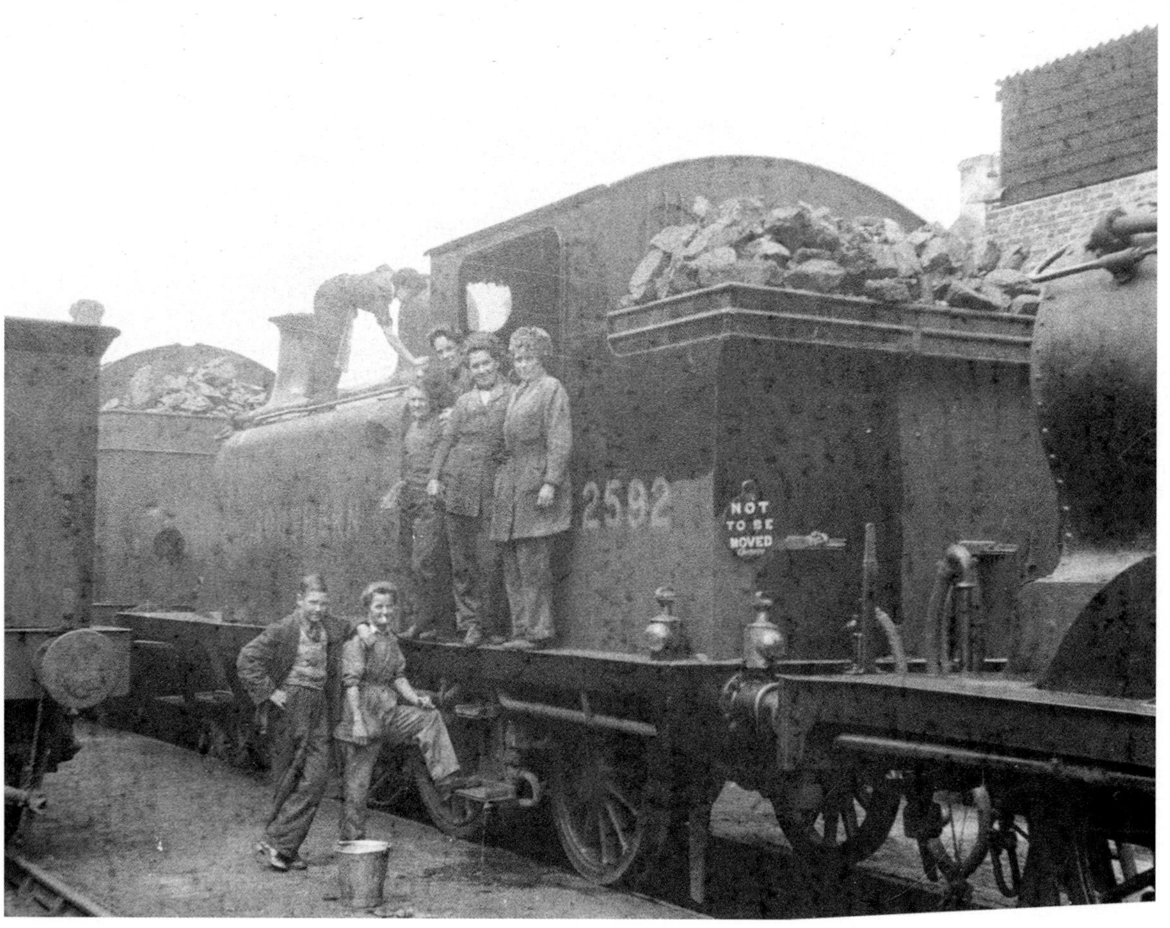
NOT
TO BE
MOVED

Opposite top: A fine portrait of ex-LBSCR 'E4x' 0-6-2T No 2478 taken at Norwood Junction shed before the outbreak of war in 1939. The engine, designed by Robert Billinton, left Brighton Works in November 1898 as 'E4' No 478 carrying the name *Newick*. In May 1909 it was one of four of the seventy-five strong class rebuilt by D E Marsh with a higher-pitched 4'6"-diameter 'I2' class boiler and an extended smokebox resting on a saddle. It is shown here finished in SR lined Olive Green livery and has acquired an Ashford-style flush-fitting smokebox door. Much of its time was spent at New Cross [Gate] but transfer to Norwood Junction appears to have occurred on or soon after that shed opened in 1935. It was withdrawn from Norwood in June 1956. *RCR 67*

Opposite bottom: Whilst certainly not up to the standard we later associate with Dicks' photographs, I have included this one for the sake of historic interest. The Railways had been included in the list of Reserved Occupations drawn up in 1938, preventing conscription from among them, it is known many men still left them for military service at the beginning of the War. Women like these, photographed at New Cross Gate shed, likely following the outbreak of war, took their places. Other than one particularly conscientious cleaner(?) atop the engine, all have stopped work for the moment on Billinton 'E5' class 0-6-2T No 2592 for Dick's camera to record them. But just who was the man resting a hand nonchalantly on the woman's shoulder? His clothing suggests he didn't intend to get himself dirty. *RCR 728*

This page: Dick took this panoramic view of Rotherhithe Road carriage sidings from a train on the South London Line viaduct at South Bermondsey. It is undated but would appear to be late 1939/ early 1940. The 30'-span arches of the main Brighton line viaduct hide the older London & Greenwich Railway structure while the Victorian bulk of St Francis Drake primary school in Deptford looms above them. The track in the foreground leads under the SLL to North Kent West Junction and Bricklayers Arms while that passing beneath the Brighton viaduct is the outlet to the ex-SER lines at North Kent East Junction. The stock in view appears to be mainly of ex-SECR or early Southern vintage and the sole engine with the vans is an SECR Wainwright 'H' class 0-4-4T. *RCR 727*

Left: This picture is undated but it would be interesting to know when Dick managed to obtain the image and more pertinently perhaps retain it for it shows the load behind the unidentified 'N' class 2-6-0 blasting up the 1 in 66 gradient of the ex-LCDR spur from Herne Hill to Tulse Hill is clearly military traffic. But the train is otherwise shrouded in mystery. The headcode is No 21 'Clapham Junction to Crystal Palace *via* Herne Hill and Tulse Hill'. Yet Crystal Palace cannot be reached from the route the train is taking here. And the headcode also prevents us knowing where this particular set of armaments began its journey. But then given the period of our history, secrecy was second nature. *RCR 719*

Below: 'S15' 4-6-0 No 844 proudly shows off its bulk at Feltham on 3rd July 1937, one of ten, Nos 838-47, built at Eastleigh in 1936; it emerged from the Works in October. There had been a gap of more than eight years since No 837's construction and followed the refusal of the Southern's Civil Engineer, George Ellson, to accept Maunsell's second proposal for a mixed traffic 2-6-2. Ellson had just taken up this position when 2-6-4T No 800, *River Cray*, derailed at speed near Sevenoaks on 24th August 1927 with some loss of life, leaving him with a strong mistrust of heavy engines with a leading pony truck. In this instance that refusal resulted in the dust being blown off the drawings for the 'S15' and this batch of ten appearing. No 844 spent much of its nationalised existence in the west at Exmouth Junction but was back at Feltham before withdrawal as No 30844 in June 1964. The engine is fitted with a vacuum pump worked off the nearside crosshead but these proved difficult to maintain in wartime and were removed. Note too the increasing lack of focus towards the rear of the engine, symptomatic of the point in the introduction about Dick Riley's early camera(s). *RCR 531*

Note: The headcodes referred to in this section were applicable between 1936 and 1944.

2 Through the Inner Suburbs

The last day of January 1960 and 'Scotch Arthur' No 30773, *Sir Lavaine,* leads the 12.24pm Waterloo-Basingstoke train away from Clapham Junction, its driver perhaps hoping he can accelerate quickly enough from the 40mph limit through the curvy main line platforms to beat the oncoming electric to Earlsfield. Richard Maunsell took Urie's 'N15' and by making some small but significant changes produced a first class workhorse, thirty of which, Nos 763-792, were supplied by North British between May and October 1925. At that time the Southern was the subject of major public criticism, so much so General Manager Herbert Walker appointed the journalist John Elliot to improve its image. Whether Elliot himself or one of his staff was familiar with his Malory or his Tennyson is uncertain but the naming of these engines after King Arthur's knights at that time was little short of genius. Maunsell didn't object but merely observed that naming would not make the engines run any better. Unsurprisingly perhaps, Urie's Chief Draughtsman, Thomas Finlayson, never agreed these were an improvement on the original 'N15'; to think so was solely due to unquestioning acceptance of Ashford's propaganda. *Sir Lavaine* spent the immediate post-war years at Dover but by 1953 had transferred to Stewarts Lane. Eastleigh then took it in on completion of the first stage of the Kent Coast electrification, withdrawal from there coming in February 1962. But it is fortunate someone in authority had the good sense to see the virtues of the class and saw No 777, *Sir Lamiel* – holder of a 'record' Salisbury-Waterloo run - taken into the National Collection. *RCR 14436*

But for the signalling this photograph could have been taken at almost any time from the early 1930s. In fact 'T14' class 4-6-0 No 461 is seen on 7th July 1950 passing through Vauxhall with a train almost pure South Western from front buffer beam to tail lamp and coded for Bournemouth West. Whether it went that far is uncertain though; as this is a Summer Friday it is quite possibly an 'extra' working. The engine was turned out of Eastleigh in March 1912, only months before the death of its designer, Dugald Drummond, and the penultimate member of its class. As a whole the 'T14' was the most successful of Drummond's big engines which, in the general scheme of things, isn't saying much, for the fleet-footed 'Greyhounds' and powerful 'D15's were a match for them. The massive splashers originally provided earned them the nickname 'Paddleboats' or 'Paddleboxes'. Robert Urie considered them worthy of superheating, No 461 being so equipped in March 1918, although it was left to Richard Maunsell to attempt to solve the continuing problem of overheating of the driving wheel axleboxes. No 460 was the first to have the lower line of the splashers lifted well clear of the wheel centres and to be provided with mechanical lubrication. Maunsell also fitted his own design of superheater as the Eastleigh ones required renewal. (Maunsell's had a little less heating surface but was easier to remove for inspection of the elements and flues.) No 461 received this reconstruction in June 1931. The class survived the war other than No 458, so severely damaged by a bomb while in Nine Elms shed write-off was the only option. Drummond engines had a reputation for being all but indestructible though the late Derek Cross did comment 'it was a big bomb!' Three of the class were taken over by British Railways, No 461 being the last to feel the cutters' torch, withdrawn in June 1951. Incidentally, it is common and understandable to pronounce Maunsell's name as it is spelt, *MaWnsell*. The late and much respected Alistair MacLeod, who worked for him, was always keen to point out that RELM could get very angry indeed if addressed in this way. He insisted it was pronounced MANSELL with no hint of the 'U' being recognised. *RCR 4060*

The now-preserved "Merchant Navy" 'pacific' No 35028, *Clan Line,* accelerates away from Clapham Junction with 'The Royal Wessex' on 5th April 1955. The train had come up from Bournemouth West at 8.20am with a scheduled arrival time at Waterloo of 11.8am. Though coming into service in 1945 the train was not named until 1951, in celebration of the Festival of Britain. Returning at 4.35pm it called at Winchester, Southampton Central and Brockenhurst to reach Bournemouth Central at 6.55pm. A two-hour schedule was re-introduced in 1957, matching that of the pre-war 4.30pm non-stop 'Bournemouth Limited'. In 1960 the service was extended to Weymouth, calling at Wareham, where a Swanage portion was detached, Wool and Dorchester South. That made it the heaviest timetabled train out of Waterloo, regularly loading to thirteen coaches to Bournemouth Central. (The usual maximum westward was eight.) Even then it was not unusual to find it entrusted to a 'light' pacific. *Clan Line* entered traffic from Eastleigh in December 1948 so never carried Bulleid's unusual number formation. After a spell at Dover much of its life was spent at Stewarts Lane where haulage of the 'Golden Arrow' and the 'Night Ferry' often fell its way. It was the last of the class to be rebuilt, in October 1959, and on completion of the Kent Coast Electrification Scheme went up the road to Nine Elms. Among the last to be withdrawn on commissioning of the Bournemouth Electrification, *Clan Line* was purchased in working order by the Merchant Navy Locomotive Preservation Society under whose care it worked its first revenue-earning service in 1974 between Basingstoke and Westbury. It has twice been fully overhauled by the MNLPS, which has owned the engine for almost three times as long as it ran in BR service, and remains a popular locomotive for organised tours as well as its regular haulage of the luxury "British Pullman". *RCR 6008*

Above: Former LBSCR class 'B4x' 4-4-0 No 2052, still denying it is now publicly-owned, leads a Maunsell brake 3rd in grubby carmine and cream through Vauxhall and towards Waterloo on 8th July 1950. A number of 'Brighton' engines, including several 'K' class 'moguls', were drafted in to work air-braked LNER stock borrowed to carry visitors to the Farnborough Air Show on the 7th and 8th of August, so perhaps this was something of a familiarization run prior to that occasion? This engine was turned out of Brighton Works in December 1899 as 'B4' No 52, finished in Stroudley's 'improved engine green' livery and named *Siemens*, one of a class eventually thirty-three in number. A name change to *Sussex* came in September 1908. ('B4' No 50, *Tasmania,* was painted grey and numbered 52 for an official photo in May 1923. But that engine was dual-brake fitted, the genuine No 52 having air brake only, showing the portrait was that of an imposter. Confusingly, No 72 also had the name *Sussex* until erasure under the Marsh regime.) Billinton's son Lawson began reconstruction of twelve of the thirty-three in 1922 though the Southern completed the process. Despite classification as 'rebuilds', with the standard Brighton 'x' added to the classification as confirmation, there was precious little of the originals left. No 52 underwent the process in May 1923. But they were disappointing engines, in part because they retained their motion plates and short travel valve gear. Transfer of ex-LSWR 'L12' 4-4-0s to the Central Section in early Southern days showed how poorly the 'B4x' performed, and although some work to improve them later went on at Brighton and Eastleigh they were never as competent or efficient as the 4-4-0 engines produced by either the SECR or the South Western. No 2052 was withdrawn in December 1951 though had war not intervened it is doubtful it would have survived the 1940s. *RCR 4068*

Opposite top: Dick is standing on the Heathfield Road bridge over the South Western Main line where the forbidding bulk of HMP Wandsworth looms above Clapham Cutting. An up Salisbury train passes with 'Battle of Britain' class 'pacific' No 34052, *Lord Dowding,* at its head. An anticlockwise Waterloo-Waterloo electric keeps pace for the moment but will fall back as it prepares to call at Clapham Junction. Clapham, incidentally, is over a mile from Clapham Junction which is more or less centered in Battersea. At the time the station opened in March 1863 Clapham was very much the up and coming district, Battersea quite the opposite. Deception ruled! The first 'Light' pacific – it weighed only 86 tons! – No 21C101, left Brighton Works in May 1945 and from that time production was virtually continuous until the 109th entered traffic in May 1950. There was then a hiatus of seven months before the 110th appeared, as though enough leftovers were found about the Works to complete it. The first seventy engines had Bulleid's Continental style of numbering but were later renumbered to match the rest, from 34001 onwards. The first forty-eight smacked of the lusher parts of the West Country and with few exceptions were allocated to appropriate sheds, but the next forty-two honoured squadrons and personnel associated with the Battle of Britain. Similarly, most of these began life at London or Eastern Section sheds. The final twenty reverted to the West Country other than the last two where the 'BB' insignia reappeared. Inevitably re-allocations, as the 'N15's and other older main line engines were withdrawn, saw some anachronisms. For example, No 34056, *Croydon*, spent most of its time at Exmouth Junction or Salisbury whereas 34037, *Clovelly,* was housed principally at Brighton and Ramsgate. When pictured on 24th May 1958 *Lord Dowding* was a Salisbury engine and four months away from rebuilding. Withdrawal from Salisbury came in July 1967. *RCR 11833*

Dick was round and about Clapham Cutting on 24th May 1958 and caught 'Lord Nelson' class No 30864, *Sir Martin Frobisher,* with the 3.30pm to Bournemouth West. The penultimate member of its class, No 864 left Eastleigh in November 1929 and went to Battersea (Stewarts Lane) for service over the lines of the former SECR. (It should be noted the class was not permitted into Charing Cross or Cannon Street.) Like all its brethren it transferred to the Western Section soon after the outbreak of war and the consequent cessation of Continental traffic, in its case to Bournemouth. *Sir Martin Frobisher,* for some time after nationalisation, was clothed in an experimental Apple Green livery before the BR dark green was decided upon for front line power. The engine escaped from experimentation as Maunsell sought various means to improve the performance of the class, but it was one of those involved in Bulleid's trials with multiple jet blastpipes and in particular the shape of and lipping on the chimney. As a result of these experiments the whole class was fitted with five exhaust nozzles in a ring allied to a wide-lipped, large-diameter chimney. Despite this the engines still had a reputation among many enginemen of being difficult to work, or more precisely, being difficult to fire. The grate was no less than 10'6" long, level for the half nearest the firehole door and sloping downward thereafter under a low brick arch. Their best work was probably done in their twilight years when all were concentrated at Eastleigh under the late Stephen Townroe's stewardship and firemen thus had plenty of opportunity to master the art of feeding them successfully. (As one current steam driver commented, 'we treat it [No 850] like a 'Scot'.) No 30864 was withdrawn from Eastleigh in January 1962. Incidentally, Martin Frobisher was a Yorkshireman, born in 1535, who despite his best attempts failed to find the North West Passage in 1574. But as Vice-Admiral to Drake he took part in the defeat of the Spanish Armada in 1588, which brought him his knighthood. He died of wounds in Brittany in 1594. *RCR 11835*

Left; Most unusually Dick tries a shot into the sun, this from the west window of 'B' box, to catch 'West Country' 4-6-2 no 34027, *Taw Valley*, approaching Wimbledon on 2nd March 1957 with an express from Plymouth. The engine at the time was shedded at Exmouth Junction which implies it has worked through rather than being relieved at Salisbury, though the Exeter men probably were. From the length of the train and evidence of several carriages with brake vans this may well be the 2.30pm from Exeter Central. If so it had left Plymouth Friary at 11.35am, possibly headed by an Exmouth Junction 'T9', and called at all stations around Dartmoor, arriving at Exeter St Davids at 2.5pm, perhaps to take a banker for help up the intervening 1 in 37 for an arrival at Central six minutes later. Notes in the timetable show it picks up a Refreshment Car here as well as the 'through' carriages from Torrington and Ilfracombe. Arrival at Waterloo is scheduled for 6.33pm. The engine left Brighton Works as 21C127 in April 1946, was rebuilt into more conventional form at Brighton in September 1957 and then posted just across the station approaches to Brighton shed. Perhaps this was to check all was well because it went off to Ramsgate only months later. Kent Electrification saw it transferred to Salisbury where withdrawal took place in August 1964. Having languished at Woodham's Yard at Barry for fourteen years *Taw Valley* was purchased and restored. *RCR 10290*

Opposite bottom: I imagine, despite his loyalty to his chief, Robert Urie must have been mightily relieved to find himself in a position to undo much of Drummond's later work which, as his Works Manager, I'm sure he realised from the drawing board could not match by its complication the standard of work produced by the simple, straightforward, four-coupled engines that preceded it. The 'D15's must have been welcome as well as proving a point. With the yard at Feltham nearing completion Urie's attention turned to providing a powerful engine for the heavy freight trains this concentration of marshalling could generate. To that end he produced the 'S15' 4-6-0 in March 1920, a total of twenty being built at Eastleigh up to May 1921. No 30496, pictured at Vauxhall, was the last out but the first numbered. Maunsell thought well enough of the class to produce another twenty-five with minor modifications, two batches, in 1927 and 1936. The engine carries the No 9 headcode, Waterloo to Plymouth, though it is possible the train is for Salisbury, likely fast to Woking, Basingstoke and then all stations to the Cathedral City. Appropriately No 496 was a Feltham engine for many years and was withdrawn from there in June 1963. *RCR 4072*

Above: The 12.30pm Waterloo-Bournemouth service, 'Bournemouth Belle' – note no definite article precedes the name! – climbs away through Clapham cutting behind 'Merchant Navy' class 4-6-2 No 35020, *Bibby Line,* on its 87-minute non-stop run to Southampton Central. The date is 31st January 1960. The inaugural train consisted of ten Pullmans, three being 1st Class, which left Waterloo at 10.30am on Sunday 5th July 1931 behind 'N15' class 4-6-0 No E780, *Sir Persant.* Eighty-nine minutes were allowed to the call at Southampton West (as it was then called), with another 37 minutes for the onward run to Bournemouth Central. Termination at the West station was due at 12.52pm. On weekdays in 1931 part of the train went on to Weymouth but loadings were insufficient for the practice to be continued beyond the 1931/2 winter timetable. At the post-war reintroduction in 1946 the down departure time was set at 12.30pm with a 2.35pm arrival at Bournemouth Central, the return being at 7.25pm on a 2-hour schedule. A two-hour down run for the 108 miles, including the Southampton stop, was introduced in the 1963 Summer timetable. The service was withdrawn on the commissioning of the Bournemouth electrification on 10th July 1967. *Apropos* 35020: at nationalisation many engines at Nine Elms, including *Bibby Line,* were double-crewed and three of its four guardians, driver George James and firemen George Reynolds and Albert Hooker, were selected to man SR engines 'away from home' on the 1948 Exchange Trials. Finally, with a sense of perceptiveness they did not often show, my employers posted me in late-1959 to their Wimbledon branch. The passing of 'The Belle' was the signal for the last of the lunchtime crumbs to be dusted off on to the platform and a reluctant return made to the books and ledgers. *RCR 14438*

Despite appearances Kensington is an Inner London Borough but it is also on an important cross-London railway route. Apart from heavy freight traffic passing through, cross-country services between the North of England and the coastal resorts of Kent and Sussex could be found here changing engines for onward movement, particularly on summer Saturdays. Dick was round and about Kensington (Olympia) to take advantage of this procedure on one such Saturday, 20th August 1955, and caught Brighton 'H2' No 32424, *Beachy Head,* arriving beneath the blackened signal box with the 12.30pm(SO) Hastings-Manchester London Road train. This called at St Leonard's and Bexhill before reversal at Eastbourne – dep 12.55pm – where, perhaps, another coach or two may have been added, and Brighton, where there would certainly have been an addition before No 32424 took charge for a 1.50pm departure; a second reversal occurred there of course. It is likely a Stanier 'Black 5' is waiting just out of shot to take the train forward. Stoke-on-Trent is the next noted call but no doubt another engine or crew change was due further north, at Rugby perhaps. Arrival in Manchester after a call at Stockport Edgeley was at 7.16pm. The stock is of LMS origin, having been timetabled to leave Manchester at 11.40pm on Friday and travel through the night with a scheduled arrival time at Brighton of 5.46am on Saturday morning. (One would hope the Brighton station Refreshment Room was open to serve breakfast to these hardy travellers.) It was due at Hastings at 7.14am, leaving a turnaround of 3¼ hours before the return north. This round trip would be run only during the peak part of the Summer timetable, from the beginning of July to the beginning of September. Was there an exhibition at Olympia that Saturday? Maybe so, for a District Line train possibly working the shuttle service from Earls Court is visible at the platform. *RCR 6567*

A Summer Saturdays Margate to Nottingham (Victoria) train sighs to a halt at Kensington (Olympia) behind the now-preserved 'West Country' class 'pacific' No 34092, *City of Wells.* The stock had set out from Nottingham at 12.45am, travelling up the former GCR route to London for an engine change at Kensington, to get to Margate at 6.37am. It left again at 12.28pm, calling at all stations to Whitstable &Tankerton (Chestfield & Swalecliffe Halt excepted) before reaching here by way of Factory Junction and Latchmere Junction. No 34092, being a Stewarts Lane engine, probably worked it between Kensington and Margate in both directions, retiring to Ramsgate between times for servicing. With an Eastern Region engine now on the front the train will reach ex-GCR metals at Grendon Underwood Junction by way of Acton and Northolt Junction and the joint GWR/ GCR Birmingham line. Having left this at Ashenden Junction, Woodford Halse was the next noted stop, and after further calls at Rugby, Lutterworth, Leicester and Loughborough, the train got to Nottingham at 6.24pm. This was a high season service, from the beginning of June to the beginning of September, just the sort of thing that deeply offended the good Dr Beeching. The photograph is dated 20th August 1955. *RCR 6566*

Above: Dick captured this fine picture of Brighton 'Atlantic' No 32425, *Trevose Head,* in full cry near Honor Oak Park on the 1 in 100 of Forest Hill bank. The headcode is No 28, generally known as 'Hither Green Sidings and Feltham *via* Richmond', which sort of train this most certainly is not. It did, however, signify the alternative route to Brighton that applied before the line south of East Grinstead closed. Dick makes no note as to the time or the train but the shadows indicate the sun is in the west. The date is 27th June 1952 and taking that into account and the fact the shadows are not yet that lengthy this is a late-afternoon service. No 32425 was then a Brighton-based engine so I suspect it is working home on the 5.40pm from London Bridge *via* Oxted, East Grinstead, Sheffield Park and Lewes. This was a tough assignment for such an engine. Other than Hurst Green Halt the train called at all stations from Sanderstead to Lewes, all eighteen of them, some with difficult uphill starts. Brighton is reached at 8.16pm though the engine has had a rest of nineteen minutes at East Grinstead and a rather shorter sit down of eight minutes at Sheffield Park. Of the six 'H2's, No 423 had gone in May 1949 but No 425 was one of four withdrawn in August and September 1956. This was the result of a recommendation in the report into the derailment of the leading bogie of LNER engine No 60700 at Peterborough nearly a year previously. Inspection showed that the similar design of the bogie in Marsh's 'H2's bore the same defect. As the cost of repair could not be justified in view of the age of these engines, withdrawal was the only option. Nevertheless, No 424, *Beachy Head,* lasted until April 1958 and is presently being reincarnated at the Bluebell Railway workshops at Sheffield Park. *RCR 4361*

Opposite bottom: On 3rd June 1951 Dick had taken himself to the lineside at Tooting Bec on the ex-LBSCR route between Balham and East Croydon and pictured 'U1' 2-6-0 No 31905 on the down main with a 4-car train of Maunsell stock for Oxted and Tunbridge Wells West *via* Edenbridge Town. It is frustrating that the set number on the carriage end is not quite complete but it would appear to refer to one of the 3-car sets of 59'-length vehicles turned out in April 1932. Two sets, Nos 223 and 224, were among several transferred to the Central Division in 1935 and although I can find no confirmation this is one of those, augmented to a 4-car set by this time, it is a possibility but I won't go further than that. Much more can be accurately determined about the engine, one of a class of twenty-one. The prototype was turned out of Ashford as No A890 in December 1925, the sole member of class 'K1', a 3-cylinder development of the 'K' class 2-6-4T. A very handsome engine, it featured a conjugated valve gear to drive the centre valve designed and patented in 1909 by Maunsell's Assistant CME, Harold Holcroft. Whereas the levers in Gresley's much better known gear took their drive directly from the outside valves, Holcroft used the outside combination levers as his source of motion, thus avoiding the problem of inaccuracies in Gresley's as the valves heated up and expanded. Like Gresley's however, the gear suffered from flexing of the levers and it was removed in 1931, a third set of Walschaerts gear being set between the frames instead. By that time, in common with the 'K' 2-6-4T engines, No A890 had been rebuilt at Ashford into a 2-6-0 of class 'U1'. This followed the serious derailment with the loss of thirteen lives of No A800 at Dunton Green in August 1927 and the recommendation by the Board of Trade Inspector for that reconstruction, his report having concluded water surging about in the tanks had made the engine unstable on the indifferent track. At a meeting on the morning following the accident the Southern's General Manager, Herbert Walker, had already suggested to Maunsell that might be the best course to take, the class already having a record of derailments though without such devastating consequences. No 31905 was the sixteenth member of the production series, leaving Eastleigh in August 1931. A Stewarts Lane engine for much of its life, No 31905 finished its days with nine others at Norwood Junction. Only four of the twenty-one survived the wholesale withdrawal of the class at the end of 1962; No 1905 was not one of them. *RCR 4247*

This page bottom: On 8th June 1951 Wainwright 'E' class 4-4-0 No 31273 makes a stately climb towards Forest Hill with the 5.20pm London Bridge-Tunbridge Wells West *via* Oxted and Hever, formed by a seven-coach ex-SECR 'Birdcage' set. No 273 was Ashford-built in February 1906. Though not matching the elegance of the 'D' that preceded it, the E' was nonetheless an attractive engine, even in the grimy state shown here, but especially when arrayed in Wainwright's sumptuous and flamboyant livery. A Bricklayers Arms engine, No 31273 is in its last few months of use, facing withdrawal in October. One point of note is the slender, arched, reinforced concrete bracket supporting the signals for the up slow and main lines. These had been erected for the colour-light resignalling between Bricklayers Arms Junction and Norwood Junction North commissioned on 8th October 1950. Many remain in place and some are still in use. *RCR 4240*

1003
33

Opposite top: Saturday 16th May 1959 sees Dick on the Grove Lane bridge at Denmark Hill to catch 'N1' class 2-6-0 No 31876 powering eastward with a train for the North Kent Coast. It has almost certainly started out from Victoria but the coaching set No 233 asks a question. Completed in 1932 as a 4-set of 59' stock it been increased to a 5-set in 1941 and had had two more coaches added in 1942. By the time the photo was taken it had become a 10-set specifically allocated along with set No 234 to the Birmingham-Margate service. On Summer Saturdays this would leave Birmingham Snow Hill soon after 10.0am, having made a connection with an early morning train arriving from Birkenhead Woodside *via* Shrewsbury and Wolverhampton. Travelling through Oxford and Reading took it 'the long way round' through Redhill, Tonbridge, Ashford and Canterbury. But Denmark Hill is most certainly not on that route, but then neither is it Summer. The reporting number on the smokebox door suggests then that this is an 'extra' and Set 233 happened to be conveniently placed in the berthing sidings to cover it. Note, by the way, the signal post in front of the train is devoid of arms and that the little LBSCR signal box is open to the world and unmanned. Colour-light signalling had come into use earlier that year in connection with the first stage of the Kent Coast Electrification Scheme, public services commencing on 15th June 1959. *RCR 13313*

Opposite bottom: A new 'Hastings' DEMU passes through London Bridge with the requisite '33' route code on show. But all is not quite what it seems. The date is 13th March 1957 but it will be another three months before the full diesel service comes into operation. Hence this is most likely to be a test/ training run; the instructor or Motive Power Inspector visibly occupies the offside of the cab of unit No 1003, one of the seven 'short' sets built on 58' underframes when the operation was planned as a six-coach 'dumb' set worked push/ pull by a diesel-electric locomotive. Following a reduction in Hastings Line services in the mid-1960s, three of these short sets were disbanded to form six 'new' sets for work over the North Downs Line between Tonbridge and Reading. A motor coach and a 2nd class trailer from each were allied to an 'EPB' driving trailer, the contrasting full width of that vehicle leading to the units being nicknamed 'Tadpoles'. Under the TOPS system they became class 206; all had gone by 1985. Commissioning of the electrification of the Hastings Line on Sunday 27th April 1986 saw the remaining DEMUs withdrawn though unit 1001, the first of the 'short' sets, has been preserved. *RCR 10331*

Above: Did Richard Riley wait for this or did he simply have his camera in hand as 'Schools' No 30936, *Cranleigh,* came sprinting down the 1 in 101½ gradient from Penge tunnel towards West Dulwich station with a Ramsgate-Victoria express on 15th September 1956. This was a Saturday so a reporting number on the smokebox door will identify the train for the signalmen from the working timetable. Change is in the air for the Winter timetable takes effect next weekend. No 936 was one of the last nine of the class and left Eastleigh in June 1935 and was a Bricklayers Arms engine for many years. Like most of its class it was swept away in a great swathe, withdrawn in the last two months of 1962. *RCR 7995*

Above: Downhill all the way now for 'West Country' class No 34092, *City of Wells,* as it bursts out of Penge tunnel and passes through Sydenham Hill station with an up 'Continental' that has travelled the secondary and hilly route through Maidstone East. Such steam workings have only a limited future for this is 30th March 1959 and the first stage of the electrification to the Kent Coast is only months away from commissioning. No 34092 left Brighton in September 1949 – part of Order 3486 - named as *Wells,* which it carried until the upgrade occurred in March 1950. It was never rebuilt, and, having been allocated to Stewarts Lane until the electrification was complete, moved on to Salisbury in May 1961 from where it was withdrawn in November 1964. It languished for nearly seven years in Woodham's Scrapyard at Barry before rescue and renovation at the Keighley & Worth Valley Railway. It enjoyed some main line outings and was later fitted with a Giesl ejector to improve performance and fuel consumption. As of March 2019 the locomotive was purchased by the East Lancs Railway when weight restrictions placed by the Local Authority on a bridge at Keighley made it impossible for the engine to return after a visit. *RCR 13111*

Opposite top: Borough Market Junction signal box, tucked into a seemingly precarious position above Borough High Street, stands in the shadow of Southwark Cathedral. A late friend of mine, a Signal Inspector of many years' experience, told me he once took over the duty of the signalman here but in less than half-an-hour had to give up and hand back control. Perhaps that is as good an illustration as any of the demands made on the man here – or rather two men as the box was generally double-manned. There could be no greater contrast than the attitude of the 'lookout' leaning nonchalantly against the plinth while his colleagues appear to be carrying out some sort of work on the cable duct. London Bridge Panel took over control of the junction on 16th April 1976. *RCR 5703*

Opposite bottom: 'L1' class 4-4-0 No 31785 drifts round the tight, check-railed curve into Lewisham with a train of ex-SECR stock. Its starting point is unclear but the No 3 headcode makes its destination and route perfectly so, "Hastings *via* Mid-Kent line, Oxted, Crowhurst Junction and Tonbridge". My first thought on seeing both the train and the route was a 'Hop-Pickers Special'. Any book produced by an Eastern Section engineman will usually contain some form of amusing tale about the odd, convoluted routes such special traffic took at the height of summer to keep main line paths clear. But then second thoughts took over. The date is Sunday 16th July 1950, too early for 'hopping' as the crop needs the heat and sunshine of August to ripen. Secondly, there are people on the platform dressed in what may be termed for that time 'out-for-the-day' attire and evidently preparing to board. Note the two gentlemen with the inevitable raincoat draped over the arm. (One is half hidden by the member of staff carrying a package, perhaps to pass to the engine crew.) Thirdly, the engine is not some near-wreck dragged out of the depths of the shed to meet the high demand of traffic but one of Bricklayers Arms' finest. No, the headcode may thus be taken as perfectly genuine and this is a 'cheap excursion' to the coast with more calls to make locally down the line. The train would have probably set out from London Bridge though possibly, by way of Peckham Rye and Nunhead, from Holborn Viaduct. I doubt any mention of it could be found in a published timetable but a properly printed notice would appear outside the appropriate stations two or three weeks in advance perhaps, advertising 'A Day Out to The Coast' at a cost of a few shillings. *RCR 4089*

LEWISHAM

1031
22

Opposite: The New Order! Slab-sided DEMUs began to be introduced for the Hastings route *via* Tunbridge Wells from January 1957 though it was not until 6th May that year that the first revenue earning service was run. Full operation began on 17th June. Here, unit Nos 1014 and 1031 come thumping up the 1 in 140 gradient from Parks Bridge Junction on 2nd May 1959. The train has just crossed the notorious South Circular Road at Hither Green, the extreme end of the headshunt in the down yard giving a clear indication of the steepness of the gradient. The first seven of these sixteen sets – seven others included a Buffet Car – had one compartment less in each coach than the others. The original design postulated six-coach trains worked push/ pull by a diesel-electric locomotive which made it necessary to mount the vehicles on 58'-long frames to ensure there was sufficient platform length available at the London termini. Construction had already begun when the decision was made to go for self-contained units instead and 64' frames could be used. Richard Maunsell had begun building 'O' restriction stock, to a maximum width of 8'0½", in 1929 because of the tight clearances in some tunnels south of Tonbridge. These units continued the tradition. The late Stephen Townroe tells of overnight trackwork that left a slight misalignment in one tunnel causing door handles to be ripped off as two trains passed one another in it. When the line was electrified in 1988 track through Somerhill, Strawberry Hill, Wadhurst and Mountfield tunnels was singled to permit use of standard rolling stock. *RCR 13226*

Above: On Monday 30th March 1959 'N' class 2-6-0 No 31414 is almost at the head of the climb out of the Thames Valley as it approaches Sydenham Hill with ECS. The headcode is No 8, Victoria and Ramsgate, but exactly where it will finish its journey is known now only to the operating staff of the time though likely to go the whole distance. Among points of interest is the ex-LCDR lattice signal post with its distinctive finial, but now fitted with a Southern upper quadrant arm. The lengthy train appears to be of 'Standard' stock in carmine and cream other than the two Maunsell coaches in green at its head. Ashford turned out the last of the 'Woolwich' engines in August 1925 but seven years later the Southern ordered another batch of fifteen, numbered 1400-14, the first coming into traffic in July 1932. This lot contained some detail differences. For example, they were fitted with the shorter 'N1' class chimney and smaller smoke deflectors. The last eight examples that obviously included No 1414, which left Ashford in January 1934, were built with the standard SR left-hand side driving position. The engine was a long-term Stewarts Lane resident but like many of the class it finished its days at Guildford. Withdrawal came in November 1962. *RCR 13110*

Brixton and the Catford Loop: 'E1' class No 31019 takes it with the 11.50am Victoria-Ramsgate train on Saturday 8th May 1954, Maunsell 3-coach set No 456 leading. Until arrival of the 'Schools' in 1930 I doubt any 4-4-0 in the country could match the Maunsell 'rebuilds' of classes 'D1' and 'E1'. It is probable this train is at least nine coaches long, but where else could one find an engine of such modest proportions being expected to take 300 tons or more over such a difficult road to the Coast as the Chatham? As a teenager I would sometimes cycle on a Saturday morning to the Blackbrook Lane bridge at Bickley. This gave the advantage of having both the Chatham and South Eastern main lines in view, agreed the latter at a little distance. I still carry indelible memories of these 'rebuilds' bringing ten 'full and standing' coaches up the 1 in 95 start from Bromley South and missing a heart beat or two as they passed thunderously under that bridge. Perhaps the greatest feat of haulage recorded was by 'D1' No 1145 on a troop train from Canonbury to Fleet. Nine Elms driver Bert Hooker, still a fireman then, recalls his heart sank when it arrived at Canonbury behind an LNER 'V2' 2-6-2, all fourteen, heavy LNER bogie coaches of it. Bert and his driver, Passed Fireman Charlie Sutton, arranged for the 'V2' to give them a push the length of the platform and a warning to be sent to all the signalmen not to stop them before the top of the continuous climb to Hampstead tunnel because the engine would never restart the train. Bert records No 1145 was worked flat-out, full regulator, full gear and that "the exhaust was fearsome to hear... but there was no sign of slip and in between each beat you could hear the safety valves just beginning to lift". They made it and the rise to the Thames bridge from Chelsea but baulked at the steeper climb to East Putney from the speed restricted turnout at Point Pleasant Junction. It was arranged Byfleet Junction would be reached by way of Brentford and Chertsey instead. The estimated gross load was 500 tons, the engine one-tenth of that. Gallant No 31145 was withdrawn in October 1961 while 'E1' 31019 had gone six months earlier.
RCR 5101

Factory Junction was one of Dick's preferred locations, providing as it did and still does a panoramic view in both directions. The time-honoured 11.0am departure of the 'Golden Arrow' was changed in 1952 to 2.0 pm with the sailing being from Folkestone rather than Dover though the up service continued to run from there. Here Dick has captured 'Merchant Navy' 'pacific' No 35015, *Rotterdam Lloyd,* getting into its stride after the laborious 1 in 61 climb to Grosvenor Bridge from Victoria. Note the two ordinary carriages behind the bogie luggage van. There had been periods pre-war when a downturn in the economy, particularly during the early 1930s, saw demand for Pullman comfort diminish. But this is 21st March 1959. From mid-1961 haulage passed into the care of one of the twenty-three 2,552hp 'Bo-Bo' electric locomotives built at Doncaster in 1958 and numbered from E5000. The last working of this famous train was on 30th September 1972 but by that time No 35015 had long succumbed to the cutter's torch. Put into traffic from Eastleigh in March 1945 as part of Order No HO 1189 and numbered 21C15, *Rotterdam Lloyd* ,went to Nine Elms for a few years before it passed along the Wandsworth Road to Stewarts Lane where it was based when this photo was taken. Rebuilt in June 1958, No 35015 was withdrawn from Nine Elms in February 1964. *RCR 13056*

To order a copy of an image used in this volume simply quote the page number and image position.

Above: The neat line up of locomotives on Hither Green shed confirms its primary function of handling the heavy freight traffic to and from the adjacent yards. It was completed by the Southern in 1933 and cost over £100,000 because, sitting as it does in the angle formed by the incoming Lee Spur and the main ex-SER line to Orpington, both of which are on embankments at this point, the ground had to be piled and raised by about fifteen feet to fill the void. It was dead-ended and had six roads under a northlight pattern roof as well as a raised coal stage, a wheel drop and a 65' turntable. Its opening permitted the transfer of a substantial number of freight and shunting engines from Bricklayers Arms that had previously to work down 'light' to service the yards. Identifiably on view are three 'Q1' class and three 'C' class 0-6-0s together with two of the massive 'W' class 2-6-4T as well as what appears to be another 0-6-0 in the form of a 'Q' whose wide chimney peeps over the tender of the shed's resident 'N15', No 30806, *Sir Galleron*. This engine was the last of the fourteen built at Eastleigh between March 1926 and January 1927, all were given six-wheel tenders for the Central Section after which the locomotives moved east when the main line electrifications to Brighton and Eastbourne had been completed. The photograph dates from late March 1959, also the year that the first class '33' diesel-electric engine arrived; twenty years later more than forty of the class were allocated. No 30806 was withdrawn from Eastleigh in April 1961; thirty years after that Hither Green became a maintenance base for Balfour Beatty. *RCR 13062A*

Opposite top: 'N15' 4-6-0 No 30764, *Sir Gawain,* creates the sort of atmosphere I'm sure would seriously displease the Dulwich College Estates Trustees as it forges up the 1 in 101½ to Sydenham Hill and Penge tunnel with a Chatham Line train for Ramsgate on 3rd October 1953. *Sir Gawain* was the second of the thirty 'King Arthur's - 'The Scotchmen' - turned out by North British, leaving the works in May 1925. It was a Stewarts Lane engine when photographed but following completion of the first stage of the Kent Coast Electrification it retired to the coast at Bournemouth whence it was withdrawn in July 1961. Note that West Dulwich station has recently lost its timber platforms and back fences in favour of Exmouth Junction concrete, though the original station building with its distinctive valance appears unchanged. *RCR 4831*

Opposite bottom: Canterbury Road Junction signal box viewed from a passing South London Line train. This is a typical LCDR timber structure on its steel girder frame but it is most significant because at the junction just beyond it is the end-on meeting between the Chatham and Brighton sections of the route between Victoria and Peckham Rye. In a twist of history the two companies had planned to bring lines from more or less the same point into Victoria and more or less parallel too, though some way apart. But under Parliamentary pressure they agreed that from the financial point of view and, surprisingly perhaps, from the environmental one too, running closely parallel like this would attract a less expensive first cost. The Chatham was first in the field, opening between Stewarts Lane and Herne Hill on 25th August 1862, the South London three years later. Splitting the section laterally rather than longitudinally also made equipping and maintaining it more straightforward. The Chatham had the section from Wandsworth Road Junction to this point, the LBSCR the rest eastward. The box closed on 8th March 1959 when the new Shepherds Lane power box took over its activities. That box lasted a relatively short time, the Victoria Signalling Centre assuming its duties on 29th November 1981. *RCR 4843*

JUNCTION

Above: Having climbed out of the Thames Valley with the 'Golden Arrow', 'MN' 4-6-2 No 35015, *Rotterdam Lloyd,* has had a 1¼-mile long downhill breather at 1 in 330 through Penge tunnel as it approaches Penge East on 15th May 1959. For years the all-Pullman formation has been reduced and ordinary vehicles put in place as shown by the two behind the luggage van. The arched viaduct carries the down 1854 spur from Sydenham to Crystal Palace while the bridge bearing the Brighton Main Line is visible through the arch. At Bickley Junction the train will bear away on to the newly-straightened spur to Petts Wood Junction and begin another climb, this time of 4½ miles to the summit at Knockholt. Two years on the train will be handed over to electric haulage and it will have run its full course by 30th September 1972. With electrification No 35015, will transfer back to Nine Elms from where withdrawal occurred in February 1964. *RCR 13349*

Opposite top: Adams '0395' class 0-6-0 No 30577 is seen on a gloomy Sunday 23rd November 1952 approaching Vauxhall at the head of the RCTS 'West Surrey Special', run to mark the impending closure of the Bisley branch line. The seven-coach train is made up of a 3-car set of ex-LSWR stock and two ex-Sheppey articulated twins. The engine is in the hands of driver Bert Hooker, himself an RCTS member, who commented No 30577 'ran very sweetly' and added that Guildford shed had a reputation for keeping its stock in good order. From Waterloo the train ran *via* East Putney to Brookwood where an 'M7' tank (No 30028) assumed charge for trips along the Bisley branch while No 30577 went back to Woking for 'refreshments'. The return was through Camberley and Ascot and over the Windsor Lines to Twickenham, Clapham Junction and Stewarts Lane to finish at Victoria. The three hundred or so RCTS members taking this trip must have been an especially hardy bunch as No 30577 was without steam heating apparatus, though they may have been warmed by some particularly spirited running on the return. Timers on board reported speeds of 61mph in the dip at Bagshot and 58mph at Egham at the foot of the long fall from Drake and Mounts, east of Ascot. Apparently when advised of this at the 'Trains Meeting' the following morning, the Southern Region Motive Power Officer, T. E. Chrimes, was moved to exclaim, 'Good Heavens! What was young Hooker thinking of?' *RCR 4427*

Opposite bottom: 'O1' class 0-6-0 No 31048 sets out from Beckenham Junction at 2.5pm on 30th December 1956 on the first stage of the 'Mid-Kent Railway and West End of London & Crystal Palace Railway Centenarian' rail tour. The Mid-Kent & North Kent Junction Railway, to give it its full title, opened between Beckenham Junction and Lewisham on 1st January 1857, the 'O1' taking the train over it and on to London Bridge (Low Level). There an 'E4' class 0-6-2T took over for the next stage of the journey. *RCR 10162*

3 Specials

Above: 'E4' 0-6-2T No 32472 approaches Crystal Palace from Sydenham with the 'Centenarian' which it has drawn from London Bridge. It will now take it over the WEL&CPR line which opened on 1st December 1856 to the original terminus at New Wandsworth, about a ½-mile shy of Clapham Junction. (Extension to Battersea Pier occurred in March 1858; however, Clapham Junction did not open until 2nd March 1863.) The train reversed at New Wandsworth, which had closed to passengers in November 1869 though it remained open for freight traffic, and returned at 3.44pm to Crystal Palace by way of Thornton Heath and the now-lifted spur at Gloucester Road between Selhurst and Norwood Junction. Another reversal followed at Crystal Palace, the train leaving at 4.24pm for the ten-minute trip back to Beckenham Junction. No 472 was one of the longest-lasting of its class, having come into traffic in June 1898 as *Faygate* and not being withdrawn until June 1962. *RCR 10164*

Opposite top: A Derby Day 'Pullman Special' is urged away from London Bridge by 'N1' class 2-6-0 No 31879 and spurred on towards Tattenham Corner on Wednesday 30th May 1951. (The race was won that year by *Arctic Prince*, ridden by Charlie Spares.) One of the five production 'N1's built at Ashford in April 1930, it was a Hither Green engine at this time though earlier allocation had seen it at Tonbridge because the three-cylinder layout provided a maximum width of 8'6½", making the engine slim enough to pass through the narrow tunnels on the Hastings line. Transfer to Hither Green came just before nationalisation and No 31879 continued to work from there until the Kent Coast Electrification Scheme saw it and its classmates transferred to Stewarts Lane. All six were condemned *en bloc* at the end of 1962. *RCR 4241*

Opposite bottom: It was, and still is, very rare to see a passenger train on the Lee Spur, movement usually being confined to freight traffic to and from Hither Green yard or ECS trains serviced or berthed at Grove Park. This is the RCTS London & North Kent Railtour which took place on 21st March 1959. It started at Liverpool Street and got to Blackfriars where 'E1' 4-4-0 No 31507 took over by way of Canonbury, East Finchley and Finsbury Park. The 'E1' hauled it through Woolwich to Erith and over the Crayford Spur to the Sidcup line to Lee from where it is seen making its approach to Lee Spur Junction at Hither Green. The train continued down the SER line to Chislehurst and the LCDR to Fawkham Junction to reach Gravesend West Street. From there it returned up the Sidcup line to Hither Green where Bo-Bo D8401 took over haulage to Liverpool Street *via* the Thames tunnel. (This was the first time an RCTS tour had been headed by a diesel engine.) No 31507, a longtime resident of Bricklayers Arms, was among the last of its class to be withdrawn, in July 1961. *RCR 13060*

47
31879
SPL
7

RCTS
31507
SPL
8

H
67

Opposite top: 'L1' class 4-4-0 No 31758 heads past Petts Wood Junction with what Dick recorded as a Hop -Pickers 'special' on Saturday 22nd September 1956. But I wonder. At this late date the picking would have been in full swing for about three weeks so is this perhaps a 'special' run for those left behind to make a weekend visit to their families working at the hop farms? There are, for example, no General Utility Vans for all the necessary paraphernalia the families took with them for their 'holiday', and so far as I can make out, only two guards' vans in the train. The headcode implies a run to the coast but I suspect the journey will be curtailed, possibly at Paddock Wood where branches diverged, in the one direction towards Maidstone West, in the other to Hawkhurst, though maybe a little further down into hopping country. The engine came from North British in March 1926 and at this time was allocated to Bricklayers Arms. After a period at Ashford it was, like all its classmates, withdrawn from Nine Elms, in this case in October 1959. *RCR 10020*

Opposite bottom: On 27th February 1957 a pair of Stratford-based 'B1' 4-6-0s, Nos 61280 and 61375, head towards Victoria with a Troop Special from Harwich. The train will have almost circumnavigated the Capital to get here, having joined the North London Railway at Hackney Wick Junction and then taken the former London & North Western line at Camden Town to reach West London at Mitre Bridge Junction, and *via* Latchmere Main Junction, Battersea, to where Dick was set with his camera. The line to Factory Junction curves away to the right while steam and dust shroud Stewarts Lane's monstrous 'Cenotaph' coaling plant. *RCR 10235*

Above: The Longhedge Junction signalman keeps a sharp eye on Bulleid 'pacific' No 34070, *Manston,* as it turns away towards Factory Junction with a Troop Special. The London Midland stock implies an arrival from north of the Thames but the headcode hints at a mystery as it means quite simply '*via* Maidstone East'. Therefore, the conclusion has to be that one of the many and various military installations in East Kent is about to receive a boost to its establishment. No 34070 was, appropriately, a Dover engine at this time which might also provide a clue to the ultimate destination. The engine was the last of the 'light pacifics' built before nationalisation, leaving Brighton Works in November 1947. Its final move was to Exmouth Junction whence withdrawal to Woodham's yard at Barry followed in August 1964. Following rescue and restoration it entered service on the Swanage Railway in September 2008. *RCR 13975*

4 Southern Electric

Above: Durnsford Road, Wimbledon, with a Shepperton service on the down slow being caught up by a Guildford *via* Cobham train on the down fast. In both instances the make-up is of 4-EPB units, the first of which, No 5001, appeared in 1951. But the panorama is dominated by the power station. This was built in 1915 to serve the expanding LSWR suburban electrification from its modest beginnings between Waterloo and Wimbledon *via* East Putney which opened on 20th October that year. The District had been running electric trains between East Putney and Wimbledon for ten years, supply coming from its own Lots Road Power House. The site at Durnsford Road was chosen because of the proximity of the River Wandle to provide water for the cooling towers and the sixteen boilers. These were fed from an overhead bunker supplied by a siding laid on a ferro-concrete ramp and viaduct; electric shunting engine No 74S was brought out of the depths of the Waterloo & City Line to shunt the coal wagons up the ramp to the bunkers. This is 2nd March 1957 and the little engine retains its position. The original chimney on the left was destroyed by bombing in October 1940, the one shown being its replacement; half the boilers were put out of action in the attack. When the National Grid took over the supply of electricity to the Railways the site was eventually cleared and the sheds and sidings here vastly extended to become the Wimbledon Traincare Depot. *RCR 10282*

Opposite top: Another photo from 2nd March 1957 but Dick has moved from busy Durnsford Road to quieter Strathearn Road to picture the berthing sidings and sheds of another part of Wimbledon depot. 4-SUB and 2-BIL units take second place to the ranks of 4-COR stock which, on a summer Saturday, would all be working on the Portsmouth Direct for the benefit of holidaymakers on 'The Garden Isle'. The District Line train trying to get in on the act is actually running on South Western tracks having left its own track on entering East Putney, though nowadays this section is in the hands of TfL. *RCR 10298*

A Down Portsmouth train, inevitably made up of Maunsell's ubiquitous 4-COR units, passes the neat 'Clapham Intermediate' signal box on 5th April 1955. Typical of the South Western's smaller boxes it was closed on 17th May 1936 with the first stage of the resignalling of the main line from Waterloo. The 4-CORs, introduced for express services on electrification of the 'Direct' line to Portsmouth Harbour which came into full operation on 4th July 1937, showed that some limitations displayed by the Brighton-line 6-PULs had caused changes. Now there was gangway access between sets and only four 225hp motors per four-car set which reduced the weight of the motor coaches. When compared with the 6-PUL this represented a power shortfall of about 16% per ton and frequent travelling on them during the late-1950s always gave me the impression they struggled on the long stretches of 1 in 80 that so characterised the 'Portsmouth Direct'. It may be significant too that 94 minutes were allowed for a non-stop run to Portsmouth & Southsea as opposed to the 90 minutes allowed for the 'Schools' that had preceded them hauling ten bogies. However, it is conceded this scheme was conceived at a time of economic difficulty which naturally required prudent investment. Twenty-nine 4-COR corridor sets numbered 3101-29 and eighteen 4-RES restaurant sets, Nos 3054-72, were built for the main traffic. Restaurant provision proved too lavish and the three restaurant cars written off during the war were not replaced. One peculiarity that caused staff at Portsmouth Harbour no end of trouble was the final destination shown on the roof boards, 'Isle of Wight'. How many hours must have been wasted persuading argumentative or recalcitrant passengers that Ryde could only be reached by ferry? In their latter days a few 4-CORs spent some time on Reading line services but also wandered wide, as far as Eastbourne and Dover. All had gone by the end of September 1972, though No 3142, a later set from the Mid-Sussex scheme, is preserved by the Southern Electric Group. *RCR 6007*

Above: The down end of Wimbledon station on 2nd March 1957 where 'B' box, in charge of a quite complex layout, witnesses 4-SUB unit No 4514, consisting of ex-LBSCR steam stock, working towards Holborn Viaduct *via* Streatham and Herne Hill. It is approaching the junction with the largely single-track byway that has come through Mitcham from West Croydon which place, oddly, the 4-SUB saw on its way here. Alongside 'MN' class 'pacific' No 35027, *Port Line,* works a much more glamorous duty, an express for Bournemouth. It is passing a line of Ferry Wagons standing at the 'Milk Dock' though that commodity had not been seen there for years. By this time it was receiving regular shipments of Italian motor scooters, one very probably as Dick was taking this picture. No 35027 was delivered from Eastleigh to Stewarts Lane in December 1948 before moving west to Bournemouth and then Weymouth from where it was withdrawn in September 1966 and sold to Woodham's of Barry. Rescued from there in 1982 restoration was finished in 1988. After passing through several owners/ operators it is now in the care of the Royal Scot Locomotive and General Trust. The everyday 4-SUB had gone by the end of 1958; nobody bothered to rescue that. *RCR 10288*

Opposite top: 4-SUB unit No 4317 leads another 4-car set - of Bulleid stock - on a Waterloo-Shepperton service and passes Wimbledon Yard where a 'C2x' and a couple of 'Q1's are trying to look busy. No 4317 was one of fifty-five three-coach sets ordered from Metropolitan CW&F Co. for third rail extensions on both the Eastern and Western Sections. The twenty-six sets allocated to the Western were numbered 1285 -1310 and of a design based on the ex-LSWR type having a 'torpedo' type front end design. They had one compartment less per carriage than those for the Eastern Section, a reflection of differing demand. Fitted with 300hp motors this stock was first used on the Guildford *via* Cobham service with its non-stop twelve-mile sixteen minute dash down the main line to Surbiton. As with others these sets were augmented to four cars post-war with Bulleid all-steel trailers and were renumbered 4301-25. (One set had been disbanded.) They were withdrawn between 1959 and 1961. *RCR 10293*

Opposite bottom: Unit No 4501 passes Queen's Road West signal box on a local service towards Waterloo on 26th July 1959. The inevitable disruption of traffic in wartime had shown Southern management what simple deduction should have done, the inadvisability of running eight-coach rush-hour trains made up of two 3-car units sandwiching a two-coach 'dumb' set. Post-war many of such 3-sets consisting of pre-grouping carriages were brought up to four by the addition of a Bulleid all-steel trailer. Some remarshalling of these older sets took place in the mid-1950s when the Bulleid monster was removed and tidy sets of four similar coaches were formed instead. No 4501 was an exception for it is half ex-LSWR and half ex-LBSCR and is about to pass under the former Brighton lines between Battersea Park and Clapham Junction. Two of Battersea Power Station's four chimneys loom over all. *RCR 13973*

WIMBLEDON
CLUB
4317
S

35
CHARRINGTONS

5739
35

Opposite top: On 5th May 1953 Dick photographed an empty stock movement at Knights Hill, the '35' headcode confirming it is bound for Selhurst. The 'Crystal Palace' electrification was inaugurated on 12th May 1911, the day King George V opened the Festival of Empire there to celebrate his Coronation year. The Selhurst workshops came into use in mid-1912 upon the extension of the South London Line overhead electrification at Peckham Rye to Tulse Hill and the Crystal Palace line at West Norwood Junction and Leigham Junction. However, it was some time before trains running 'light' through Norwood Junction to reach the shops actually called there in service. Expansion of the workshop site continued with extension of the overhead to Sutton and Coulsdon North *via* Selhurst in 1925 and particularly following the conversions from overhead, and installation of the third rail in 1928 between Charing Cross and the former SER Caterham and Tattenham Corner branches. It remains a major maintenance and inspection facility with the original nine-road o/h shed still in use. *RCR 4519*

Opposite bottom: Another example of ECS working to Selhurst with the '35' headcode; 2-EPB set No 5739 leads an empty train from London Bridge past Old Kent Road signal box. This is typical of the London, Brighton & South Coast Railway's smaller boxes, most of which were timber-built, though here of a timber cabin on a brick base. It features decorative valances and the ornamental finial above the ventilator. The lines going off to the right lead to Deptford Wharf and New Cross Gate, though the connections were taken out of use in November 1964. The junction was re-established in December 2012 when a link to the East London Line, originally closed in 1911, was re-opened south of Surrey Quays after much major engineering work had been completed. It filled in the last piece of the London Overground 'circle', Clapham Junction to Clapham Junction, though it is not operated in this way. *RCR 10252*

This page: The New Order, the first BR 'standard' stock built for 'Southern Electric'; 2-EPB unit No 5701, is only weeks old as it calls at Queen's Road Peckham working a South London Line London Bridge-Victoria service on 4th March 1954. This was the first of seventy-nine units built principally to increase train length on Eastern Section rush-hour trains from eight coaches to ten after the experimental 'double-deck' sets failed to impress. The large gap between the tracks here shows where an additional up line of rails between Peckham Rye and South Bermondsey Junction was once in place. This had been taken out of use in 1933 but had not been immediately removed. Station reconstruction was undertaken at the end of the 1950s to provide a wide island platform on the abandoned track bed to supersede the two narrow ones here, those at Peckham Rye and South Bermondsey being similarly treated though the latter station was moved to the south of the junction. *RCR 5036*

Above: West Norwood Junction is approached by a Victoria-Beckenham train on 1st March 1953. The 4-SUB unit is one of the 4355-77 batch introduced in 1947/8, identifiable by the grab handles above and beside the cab windows. For some reason these units reverted to all-compartment stock, a retrograde step after its immediate predecessors had set a precedent by providing more comfortable saloons as a counter to the very narrow compartments in Bulleid's first ten all-steel units Nos 4101-10. The line curling away to the right leads to Tulse Hill, the junction for lines to Herne Hill and Victoria, and Peckham Rye and London Bridge. *RCR 4428*

Opposite: Dick occupied this same viewpoint at Tooting Bec five years earlier (see page 22) and though things appear much the same the semaphore signals have gone; colour-lights superseded them in late 1952. The photograph is of a typical 'fast' coast-bound train of '6-PUL/6-PAN' stock, the leading set dating from the Brighton Line electrification in 1933. The order for forty-six motor-coaches was divided equally between Birmingham RCW and Metropolitan Cammell after each company had supplied a prototype, the one from the latter company providing the pattern for the production run. They were of all-steel construction, each fitted with four 225hp traction motors from BTH, and weighed 59 tons. Standing on the platform at East Croydon as one of the non-stop London-Brighton 'on the hour, in the hour, every hour' services went through at the regulation 40mph showed how those heavy carriages pounded the track though the trains were very lively performers. However, regular travellers soon learned to avoid the motor coaches for the riding over any track imperfections could set them lurching and bouncing, sometimes quite alarmingly. Trailer coaches were to Maunsell's standard designs on steel underframes, while twenty-three all-steel 'Compo' Pullman cars were supplied by MCW. The stock was made up into twenty six-car sets numbered 2001-20 and classified '6-PUL', and three '6-CIT' sets, Nos 2041-3, with all-1st trailers for the 'City Limited' Brighton-London Bridge commuter services. Seventeen similar '6-PAN' sets were built for the Eastbourne and Hastings electrification of 1935 but using English Electric motors, and a Pantry 1st in place of the Pullman. The '6-PUL/6-PAN' formation became common thereafter. The No 16 headcode seen here shows Littlehampton to be the destination, avoiding Brighton by way of the Cliftonville Spur between Preston Park and Hove. After some modification for a brief flirtation with the Kent Coast lines all these units had gone by the end of 1967. *RCR 6616*

3017
16

WAY OUT
5710
2
WAY OUT

4630
06
GIPSY HILL

Opposite top: BR 'Standard' 2-EPB unit No 5710 stands in the rather rundown station at Mitcham while working a Wimbledon-West Croydon service on 13th March 1955. For years unique in having number rather than letter headcodes, the stock on this line was always known as '2 trains' and the driver evidently saw no reason to change that information on the rear of the set. After all, the oil lamp with its red aspect is in the proper place. Between Mitcham and Waddon Marsh the line follows the route of the Surrey Iron Railway, the world's first public railway, opened on 26th July 1803. (Their paths cross on the approach to West Croydon.) Indeed 'Tramway Path' runs for about 400 yards along the west side of the line here. Nowadays trams coincidentally connect Mitcham and Croydon, the 'tramstop' being to the west of the station and immediately accessible. ***RCR 5680***

Opposite bottom: The first new suburban electric stock since 1925 was in the form of a 4-SUB unit produced by Bulleid in 1941. Numbered 4101 it was of welded steel construction with the bodysides a continuous curve to the maximum limit of the loading gauge to permit of six-a-side seating. Each motor coach had nine compartments of very narrow dimensions with eleven in one trailer and ten – six 1st flanked by two lots of two 3rd – in the other. Before it entered service 1st class was abolished on suburban lines so the composite was never used as such. Another nine sets, 4102-10, came into service in the last two years of the war and very soon the class gained the title 'Queen of Shebas'. (We are told she came with 'a very great train'; it offered 468 seats.) Waterloo soon began to receive complaints about the narrowness of the compartments making it difficult not just to stand but to enter and leave because passengers were seated with knees all but interlocked. Notice was taken, for the next sets produced, nos 4111-20, lost one compartment from each coach. But for the first time the motor coaches no longer had the domed front end and instead a slightly bowed and upright front featured. The wood and canvas roofs vanished too. Units Nos 4121-30 arrived late in 1946 but with saloons instead of compartments – two of four bays each in the motor coaches, and three-four-three in the 3rd trailer. (Compartments were retained in the 'compo'.) Unit No 4630, seen arriving at Gipsy Hill, was one of a batch of forty-six sets constructed in 1949 on frames salvaged from withdrawn 3-SUB sets. By this time the interior layout had become an eight-bay saloon in the motor coaches and a ten-bay saloon in one of the trailers with ten compartments retained in the other. The '06' headcode applies to the long established Victoria-Holborn Viaduct service that ran *via* Crystal Palace, West Croydon, Sutton, Wimbledon, Streatham and Herne Hill. ***RCR 14396***

Above: Of the stock provided for the Central Section electrification in 1928, some was converted from seven-coach steam-hauled sets which had been displaced by the overhead electrification to Sutton and Coulsdon North in 1925. On 11th March 1954 one of these three-car sets, with the Bulleid trailer added after the war, arrives at Crystal Palace on a London Bridge-London Bridge circular working *via* Sydenham and Tulse Hill. Commissioning of the branch from Sydenham and the palatial station at its end on 10th June 1854 coincided with the re-opening of the Crystal Palace by Queen Victoria on its new site at the top of Sydenham Hill. The approach is guarded by 'East' box, one of three here and of the earliest Brighton design; it became 'C' box after nationalisation and closed in July 1969. ***RCR 5054***

Above: 4-SUB unit No 4348 passes Bickley Junction signal box on an Orpington-Holborn Viaduct *via* Herne Hill working. This was one of fifty-five three-carriage sets ordered from Metropolitan Carriage & Wagon Company for the electrification programme in 1925. Twenty-six of these, Nos 1285-1310, were for the Western Section while the twenty-nine for the Eastern Section, Nos 1496-1524, had one compartment more per coach, symptomatic of greater demand in South East London. Post-war the sets were strengthened by the addition of a Bulleid all-steel trailer, the second coach in this train, and renumbered, the Eastern sets becoming Nos 4326-54. Incidentally, the headcode is slightly erroneous; the white dot should not be there, a problem that disappeared with the introduction of numerical codes. *RCR 10011*

Opposite: Is the Camberwell signalman more concerned with watching Dick take this photograph of a train for West Croydon *via* Wimbledon and Sutton than acknowledging the driver peering up at him? Set No 4342 is another of the twenty-nine numbered 1496-1524 ordered from Metropolitan Cammell in 1925 for the Eastern Section electrification. They were originally fitted with 'MCB' automatic couplers within the units but these were removed after a number of breakaways and the usual semi-permanent three-link couplings installed instead. After the war all these units were provided with an all-steel Bulleid trailer as shown here. *RCR 10262*

CAMBERWELL
4342
P

Above: A Bulleid 4-SUB unit on an Orpington-Victoria working passes the new power signal box at Shortlands Junction on 2nd August 1958. However, the box in the background continued in use until the colour-light installation from Beckenham Junction and Ravensbourne to Swanley was brought into use on 31st May 1959. The Victoria Panel took control of the area on 20th June 1982, meaning the original box which, incidentally, never carried the 'Junction' suffix, had control here for more than three times longer than the power box that succeeded it. Such is progress. *RCR 12566*

Opposite top: Bulleid 4-SUB unit No 4382 sets out from Holborn Viaduct on its roundabout hour-long journey to West Croydon *via* Tooting and St Helier. Having rested for about twenty minutes it will set off all stations to Victoria by way of Crystal Palace and Streatham Hill. Is it ironic that by so doing it will have travelled in a single journey on one of the youngest and also on part of one of the pioneer lines on the Southern system, the Wimbledon & Sutton Railway of 1930 and the London & Croydon of 1839. Holborn Viaduct is no more of course, but the line diving down to the left is very much alive though not quite as shown here. The train is crossing the contentious bridge over Ludgate Hill, removed to the relief of the City Fathers when the Thameslink project proposed instead to tunnel under the road and provide a new station there with access from it. After a closure to them of more than seventy years regular passenger trains had once again begun running through the Snow Hill tunnel in May 1988, but it was closed again for four months to permit the changed routing to go in, reopening on 29th May 1990. St Paul's Thameslink, though soon changed to City Thameslink to avoid confusion with the Central Line's St Paul's station at the top of Ludgate Hill, opened with this new section of route. *RCR 13057*

Opposite bottom: 4-SUB No 4723, forming a train from Sevenoaks *via* Swanley and the Catford Loop, crosses Ludgate Hill and enters Holborn Viaduct. The station opened on 2nd March 1874 though Ludgate Hill station in the background, which had opened in June 1865, continued in use until March 1929. The lines to the right lead down to Snow Hill tunnel where the low level Holborn Viaduct station was situated between August 1874 and June 1916. The St Paul's Thameslink station opened on or about its site in 1990 and Holborn Viaduct closed. Even though the photograph was taken in May 1954 there is still much evidence of wartime damage. *RCR 5093*

06

83

Above: On 6th April 1953 New Cross sees the arrival of set No 4252 leading an eight-car train for Hayes *via* the Ladywell Loop, thus avoiding Lewisham. No 4252 was originally formed as a 3-set of LBSCR steam stock displaced by third-rail electrification of the Central Section suburban services in 1928. Numbered 1631-57, most of the twenty-seven sets in this class were mounted on recovered plate underframes. Like almost all other 3-sets augmentation by a Bulleid all-steel trailer came post-war, but from the mid-fifties this series lost these and received instead ex-LBSCR coaches from withdrawn sets. At the same time they were renumbered into the 45xx series. Withdrawal dates from 1959. *RCR 4454*

Opposite top: The slight easing in the climb from Bromley South is shown as a Victoria to Sheerness train, led by 2-HAP unit No 5605, overtakes 4-SUB No 4385 on a Holborn Viaduct-Sevenoaks *via* the Catford Loop and Swanley service preparing to call at Bickley. Three generations of Southern electric stock are illustrated with brand new CEP coaches for the Kent Coast scheme berthed in the down siding. The scheme has also seen a change in use of the lines here, the Sheerness train being on what had been the Up fast until two weeks before Dick took this picture on 13th June 1959. *RCR 13623*

Opposite bottom: Led by No 2627, four 2-HAL units, about the most uncomfortable outer-suburban stock it was possible to design, pass Shortlands signal box on a Maidstone East-Victoria working on 2nd August 1958. Introduced in July 1939 for the Gillingham/ Maidstone West electrification, the seventy-six units numbered 2601-76, although of all-steel construction, were at base the same as the excellent Maunsell 2-BILs but in all else completely different. The motor coaches were compartment vehicles, unlike those in the BILs, and only the composite driving trailers were provided with a side corridor and lavatories. Towards the end of 1939 another sixteen sets numbered 2677-92 were built for the Western Section to strengthen the Reading line trains from six to eight carriages in the peaks. Commuting from Egham for a number of years made me avoid them like the plague - so far as was possible. Almost all sets were withdrawn by the end of 1970 though six survived for two more seasons to handle Christmas parcel traffic; the last went in early 1972. *RCR 12553*

90
83
SHORTLANDS
94

In the grim post-war surroundings of inner London, a 4-SUB unit of ex-Brighton stock with a Bulleid all-steel trailer passes the imposing Loughborough Junction signal box working a Holborn Viaduct-West Croydon service. This travelled by the roundabout route through Herne Hill, Tulse Hill, Wimbledon and Sutton. At West Croydon it would usually assume another identity, perhaps after a short layover, and go on to Victoria calling at all stations *via* Crystal Palace (Low Level). In later years, when Bulleid stock had ousted the ancients, the headcode was number '06'. The 'Wimbledon and Sutton Railway' had been mooted as far back as 1910, with the District to work it by extension from its terminal platforms at Wimbledon. For the moment war put it on hold. Extension of the City & South London line from Clapham to Sutton had later threatened but the Southern objected on the grounds the C&SLR was going beyond its remit. The company was, however, reluctant to build the W&SR itself. But with an aggressive Parliament hovering varied agreements were reached which, among others, curtailed the C&SLR at Morden and obliged the SR to fill the gap. It did so in parts, opening the line throughout on 3rd January 1930. *RCR 5058*

5 Portraits

Ex-LSWR Urie 'G16' class 4-8-0T No 30495 takes a break from pushing wagons over the hump at Feltham. A continual rise in the volume of freight traffic at the beginning of the 20th century caused the London & South Western Railway to look for a way to relieve pressure on Nine Elms as well as to take on much of the marshalling work carried out by the LNWR on its behalf at Willesden. The greenfield site on the south side of the 'Windsor' lines at Feltham was purchased in two parts, in 1911 and 1915, the yard being completed in 1921 though the first bank of sidings had been brought into use in December 1917. The primary marshalling was by means of gravity from humps, four 'G16' engines numbered 492-5 being built for this work at Eastleigh in 1921. At that time the Motive Power depot to service them and other engines working in and out of the yards had still to be finished so first allocation was to the nearby Strawberry Hill depot. As provision of the 65' turntable and the mechanical coaling plant were not approved until the end of 1922 the shed clearly did not become fully usable until after Grouping, perhaps as late as 1924, though Strawberry Hill had closed before the end of 1923 for transformation into an EMU berthing and service depot. No 492 was withdrawn in 1959 and the others had all gone by the end of 1962. ***RCR 14391***

Above: The enginemen on board 'C2x' class No 32553 appear to be taking it easy despite the ugly face of 'Q1' 0-6-0 No 33017 glaring at them among the ashes in Wimbledon Yard. One of no 17's classmates is also in attendance giving mutual support, and all the while a member of the Engineering Department quietly wields his paintbrush on the water tank. The 'C2x' is a Bricklayers Arms engine and has probably come down through Peckham Rye, Streatham and Tooting. It may have a trip working to St Helier on its Duty Card but will return this way for fear of failure on 'The Wall of Death' approach to Sutton. No C17 (33017) was the first of its class to be at Ashford, in May 1942, but spent most of its time on the Western Division, on this day, 2nd March 1957, based at Nine Elms from whose yard it has come. Withdrawal was from Three Bridges in January 1964, the 'C2x' having gone two-and-a-half years earlier. *RCR 10296*

Opposite top: Drummond '700' class 0-6-0 No 30696 must feel itself rather overwhelmed at Feltham shed by the presence of at least two of Urie's 'S15's. Dubs of Glasgow built the thirty engines in the class between March and June 1897. As was customary with South Western stock provided by outside manufacturers, the class was not identified by the Order Number given to the Works – 'S15' is an example – but by the number of the first engine. Except in the case of the '700' it wasn't! Like most pre-Grouping companies the LSWR often gave new engines vacant numbers in the stocklists, which made identifying the class of a loco by its number a trifle hazardous. Neither did it help that Drummond had a *penchant* for renumbering without apparent reason or logic. The '700's were originally in a nice tidy list, 687-718. But in mid-1898 Nos 702-715 became 369/15/7/25/7/39/46/50/2/5 and 368. No 716 became 459 but in June 1912 was renumbered again, to 316. I suppose it all had a purpose but the record keepers must have been kept on their toes. Like all its classmates No 696 was superheated, this engine by the SR in September 1926, and went to the breakers from Feltham in August 1961. *RCR 14034*

Opposite bottom: With Feltham yard under construction Robert Urie turned out five class 'H16' 4-6-2Ts in 1921/2 to handle freight transfer traffic to other yards, mainly those of companies north of the Thames. They were nicknamed 'Green Tanks' whereas their 4-8-0T brethren for work in the yard itself were 'Black Tanks'. In essence this was the 'S15' tender engine though it had a smaller boiler to keep it within the permitted axle-loading. Even so it weighed no less than 96½ tons in working order. No 520 was the last of the five. Though they concentrated on their principal duties, at least one could later be found on ECS work. This was not restricted to the short hops between Waterloo and Clapham Junction but also to the out-of-town Oatlands or Chertsey sidings. No 30520 is seen with the empty stock of the 'Bournemouth Belle' at Queen's Road on 26th July 1959. All five of the class were withdrawn in 1962. *RCR 13968*

30696
30696
PULLMAN
30520

The necessary but the far from glamorous burden of taking heavy unbraked freight trains across London also came to rest on the broad shoulders of Maunsell's 'W' class 2-6-4T, epitomised by No 31911 of Hither Green shed at Kensington on 18th August 1956. The Southern did well out of these engines for virtually every part was available from stock. Essentially a tank engine version of the 'N1', though with a slightly larger cylinder diameter, the tanks, cabs and bogies were salvaged from the ill-fated 'Rivers'. No 31911 was the first of the five built at Eastleigh in January 1932; these had right-hand drive as was common on the SECR. Ironically, the ten built at Ashford in 1935/6 had Eastleigh-style left-hand drive. The class survived the swingeing cuts in steam locomotive numbers at the end of 1962, No 31911 being one of the last two withdrawn, in October 1964. Incidentally, note the flat wagon with the container creeping into shot, a sight not seen nowadays, not in this form anyway. ***RCR 7946***

A remarkably clean 'C2x' No 32544 butts up against the down end of Norwood Junction's platform 1. The line on which it stands is the outlet from the Up side yard and the necessary crossover to the Up Slow line is visible in the photograph. It was always a thrill as a child to find one of these engines patiently waiting here for the ground signal to clear and even more thrilling if it did so and this gruffest of beasts 'wooffed' past the windows of the booking hall with its thirty or so protesting wagons in tow and the grinding brake van bringing up the rear, sometimes with the guard leaning nonchalantly over the back rail. But this time it appears to be going nowhere with the steel 'hopper' against its buffer beam and the driver gazing into space. No 544 left Vulcan Foundry as a 'C2' in December 1901 and in January 1911 became one of the earliest to be rebuilt into class 'C2x'. A longtime resident of Norwood it was withdrawn in November 1961, a month short of its 60th birthday and ten years after being pictured by Dick's camera. *RCR 4322*

Above: "A collection of 'K's" at Norwood Junction on 11th May 1958, having escaped from their home shed at Three Bridges. A beautifully clean No 32342 and rather grubby No 32346 were the first and last of the five authorised by the Government during the First World War in view of the success of the original five, being produced in October and December 1916 respectively. No 32348 was the second in a subsequent order for ten, leaving Brighton Works in December 1920, though after seven had been put into traffic a halt was called to erecting the others until a backlog of repairs had been tackled. Maunsell, having settled on his own 'N' class as 'standard', cancelled them, supposedly on the basis the 'K' was more difficult and costly to maintain. That was a pity as it was relatively trouble-free and at speed behaved rather better than the Maunsells did. For political reasons all seventeen of the class were, like many other steam engines when the British Transport Commission handed its responsibilities to the British Railways Board, withdrawn *en bloc* at the end of 1962. *RCR 11809*

Opposite top: A pair of 'C2x's nose to nose at Norwood Junction in April 1960, each having just eighteen months service left. Being among the last batch of 'C2' class engines built by Vulcan Foundry, both came into service in January 1902. They were naturally among the forty-five members of the fifty-five-strong class rebuilt with the larger 'C3' boiler to become 'C2x'. However, while No 547 received the upgrade in August 1908 No 548 had to wait until Grouping as the Southern continued the process, being rebuilt in March 1925. Was there an overabundance of 'C3' boilers in the boiler park at Brighton Works that caused a triumvirate to receive one after a hiatus of fourteen years? Nos 527 and 535 were so treated in October and December 1939 and No 526 in June 1940. Note that No 548 has a boiler with two domes, the one nearer the chimney once housing Lawson Billinton's top feed. When the clacks were removed to the usual position on the boiler's centre line, the dome remained to cover the plugs. *RCR 14664*

Opposite bottom: Billinton 'E6' class 0-6-2T No 32413 rests under cloudy skies at Norwood Junction shed. This class of twelve was the last and at 61 tons the heaviest of Billinton's four 'radial' classes. It was also the only one of them not to have the 18" diameter cylinders later lined up to 17½". No 413 left Brighton Works in July 1905, liveried in goods green and bearing the name of one of the first 'Terrier' 0-6-0Ts, *Fenchurch.* Robert Billinton – 'Uncle Bob' to his staff, behind his back anyway – died in office on 7th November 1904 when only one had gone into traffic. He had planned the last two engines to be finished as 0-8-0T engines specifically for the heavy yard shunting duties at Brighton's Lower Yard and at Willow Walk, heavy fluted coupling rods having specially been made for them. But Douglas Earle Marsh, who succeeded him from 1st January 1905, had them built as the rest of the class though these heavy rods were still fitted. Marsh also ended the Brighton tradition of naming every engine, hence the final four were nameless. This engine spent the postwar years at Norwood though withdrawal in November 1958 was from Bricklayers Arms. It was almost inevitable a Norwood 'C2x' would get in on the act although No 32446 appears to hide its face in shame, while a Brighton 'mogul' courteously retains its anonymity. *RCR 7879*

Portraits

32447
32447

32102

Opposite top: Norwood Junction's 'C2x' class 0-6-0 No 32447 allows its crew and the shunter a few moments rest while permitting Dick's camera to photograph it when shunting the yard at Crystal Palace on 12th March 1954. (It is likely the shunter was also the guard.) The number 10 headcode confirms the train started at Battersea Yard and is scheduled to complete its journey at Norwood's down yard once it has finished here. The canopy over the road side of the goods shed may be seen in the right background where passenger stock is berthed in the sidings alongside the branch from Sydenham, while the Permanent Way staff appear to have been recently provided with a new Exmouth Junction concrete-built hut. No 32447, one of ten of its class at Norwood at the time, was in a batch of nine numbered 445-452 that left the Vulcan Foundry between July and November 1894. Rebuilt to 'C2x' in January 1911, withdrawal came in February 1960. ***RCR 5047***

Opposite bottom: Lawson Billinton had been *de facto* in charge of Brighton Locomotive affairs for some months while D. E. Marsh was on sick leave, before being confirmed in the top position on 1st January 1912. While still in the 'acting' post he had been carrying out the Board's principal directive to concentrate on maintenance and overhaul of the stock. Having satisfied that demand and brought the last of Marsh's planned engines into being he produced five small 'E2' class shunting tank engines between May and December 1913 as replacements for some of Stroudley's 'E1' class. No 32102 was the third of these, pictured at Stewarts Lane with a rather bored-looking crew on 1st March 1959. This was one of those transferred to the Eastern Section in the mid-1930s for shunting at Herne Hill sidings and empty stock work in and out of Victoria. Southampton Docks had a taste of them from about 1955 though their use throughout that system was precluded by the relatively lengthy wheelbase and the Docks' tight curves. The class was extinct early in 1963. ***RCR 13038***

This page bottom: Plenty of time for conversation; 'H' class 0-4-4T No 31533 overhears secrets in company with a Brighton'C2x' and an SECR 'N' at Bricklayers Arms on 14th March 1959. Wainwright ordered a total of sixty-six 'H' class engines but only sixty-four were constructed during his period in office, the first six appearing from Ashford in November 1904. It was Maunsell who by various means discovered the order had not been completed and set the cat among the pigeons by insisting that it should be. The result was that Nos 184 and 16 appeared respectively in April and July 1915. No 533 came into traffic in July 1905 and was one of the forty-five members of the class to be 'motor-fitted', in its case as late as March 1960. Transfer to Tunbridge Wells West shed followed, withdrawal from there being in September 1962. No 263 of May 1905 is preserved at the Bluebell Railway. ***RCR 13041A***

Three Wise Men at Stewarts Lane in 1954 with 'E1' class 4-4-0 No 31019 forming a backdrop. In the centre stands the young but already very experienced Shedmaster, Richard 'Dick' Hardy, then only about thirty years of age but, as he admitted, 'looking older'. After a Premium Apprenticeship at Doncaster he learned his managerial trade around the LNER under the guidance of the formidable Leslie Preston Parker and admitted he applied for Stewarts Lane because he'd let King's Cross pass, 'a silly thing to do'. In 1964 he was plucked out of Motive Power into General Management to become in 1968 Divisional Manager at Liverpool for five years before a move to Marylebone Road. He finished his working life by supervising the career development of graduates coming into the industry. But he remained a loco man at heart and nothing pleased him more than footplating and firing a steam engine. On Dick's right stands Fred Pankhurst, Chief Running Foreman, a rough diamond but a 'kind and loyal man' and one of remarkable memory. Dick notes Fred knew all the engine workings without reference to the diagrams just as he knew the route knowledge of every man in the depot. Perhaps more remarkably still, he knew the inner workings of other depots and their 'hidden' spare engines, in particular at Bricklayers Arms, where he had worked before. On Dick's left is the burly figure of driver Sam Gingell, a unique man among many unique men though Dick did not consider him outstanding as a driver but did most certainly as a man. He started his working life in the Abergorky pit in South Wales and thought nothing of cycling back to the family home in London for a long weekend so as to save the train fare. He was a late-starter on the railways, joining the SECR at twenty-one years of age but gained his driver's qualifications only twenty-two years later. On retirement he had an unblemished record – bar a pencil note about making smoke at Holborn Viaduct in 1919 - and immediately took up portering at Victoria. What men these were. ***RCR 4903***

6 Non-Passenger

Not on the Southern at all for this is Kensington with the East Croydon-Wood Lane Milk empties passing through behind 'H' class 0-4-4T No 31261. The first six-wheeled tank trailers were made by R A Dyson & Co. of Liverpool for the Co-operative Wholesale Society in 1931 and originally had solid tyres. They were transported on 4-wheel trucks built at Lancing, the Southern being the first company to introduce them. But these were soon found to ride poorly at speed and were superseded by 6-wheel trucks produced in 1932. The Southern served several bottling plants in the London suburbs but the main discharge point was at Vauxhall where pipes under the platform took the milk to the plant in the arches. For many years empties were worked back to the West Country from the Windsor side of Clapham Junction at 3.54pm, a very heavy train often requiring the power of a 'Merchant Navy' engine. Even then the services of an 'M7' were regularly needed to assist it up the steep climb to East Putney from the speed-restricted turnout at Point Pleasant Junction. Photographed on 18th August 1956 No 31261 left Ashford Works in November 1905 as No 261, it had the 'A' for Ashford and the later 1000 added before the 30000 of BR. Many years allocation to Stewarts Lane were concluded with withdrawal from there in October 1961. ***RCR 7947***

Dick adopted a potentially perilous position under one of the arches of the Trinity Road bridge at Wandsworth though he was possibly in less danger there than among the traffic on it. An 'N15' whose number he did not note (possibly No 30789 *Sir Guy*) approaches Clapham Junction on the Up Main with a long train of vans. The head code is No 18 which has the intriguing route identification, "Light engines and trains requiring to run to Up Main Loop, Clapham Junction, from stations westward". No hint then of the train's starting point though the signalmen were much less concerned with that than the destination. *RCR 6006*

Framed by a phalanx of post-war housing, 'M7' class 0-4-4T No 30320 trundles a Van 'B' and eight milk tanks towards the Windsor side of Clapham Junction for inclusion in the late-afternoon train returning the empties to the West Country. (This train ceased to run after 6th September 1964, instead being diverted to the WR main line.) The Southern introduced its first fixed milk tank wagons in 1931, using 4-wheel trucks as it had for the milk tank trailers, though six-wheelers soon superseded them. Someone in authority clearly concluded that if a six-wheel tender full of water ran steadily behind an engine, six wheels would provide the same steady ride for a full tank of milk. (With less oscillating compared with a four-wheel chassis, milk with a high fat content was also less likely to start turning to butter en-route.) It should be noted that while the railway owned the truck the tank was the property of the dairy company. Queen's Road signal box stands in the shadow of the viaduct carrying the Brighton lines from Victoria, marooned within a sea of track, the two nearer ones being the South Western's up and down slow lines. The engine was one of five built at Nine Elms in 1900 to Order B10, coming into traffic in August, and was withdrawn from Nine Elms shed in February 1963. ***RCR 13969***

A Peckham Rye to Lillie Bridge freight, consisting almost entirely of former private owner timber-bodied open wagons, climbs the spur to Leigham Junction behind ex-SECR 'C' class 0-6-0 No 31724. Though they co-operated in opening and maintaining the coal depot at Peckham Rye as a joint venture, the rivalry for Scottish traffic made the Midland and LNWR rather uneasy bedfellows. Traffic to and from the yard was worked over the West London Railway and its Extension. This view, taken on 11th March 1954, is much changed now with the closure of Tulse Hill's coal depot– seen on the right – and the growth of trees alongside the track over the last half-century. But all is still overlooked by the tapering spire of Holy Trinity church. ***RCR 5041***

Above: The 12.4pm 'vans' is ready to set out for East Croydon, Redhill and Tonbridge behind 'E1' class 4-4-0 No 31497, following the original SER route to Dover. It is standing in the 'Low Level' part of London Bridge station approximately in the space occupied by the terminus of the London & Greenwich Railway, the first into London, opened from Spa Road on 14th December 1836. The London & Croydon obtained this in 1844 in a swap with its own station to the north of the location. Late into BR days it remained rather isolated with the higher level 'through' lines on one side and the massive yellow-brick wall of the Brighton station on the other. The engine, a development of the earlier 'D' class, came into service as 'E' class No 497 in September 1907, Beyer Peacock rebuilding it with a superheater boiler in June 1920. Barely two years into service No 497 was hauling an express passenger train when the driver overran signals at Tonbridge and collided with a mail train headed by sister engine No 165. There were two fatalities. Repaired, and later as No 31497 the engine was based at Bricklayers Arms for much of its career, being withdrawn from that shed in October 1960. ***RCR 5110***

Opposite page: Norwood Junction's 'C2x' class 0-6-0 No 32445 heads home with a freight from East Grinstead but has still to shunt the yard at Selsdon before the day's work is done. This line, from South Croydon and originally proposed in 1855 – argued over, started, abandoned and then restarted – was not finally opened until March 1884 and then as a joint enterprise by the Brighton and South Eastern as far south as Crowhurst Junction whence the Brighton had sole ownership. Selsdon had a substantial yard of five lengthy sidings as well as an oil terminal established by the Anglo-American Oil Company in 1894. Despite closure of the goods yard in October 1968 the terminal continued to function until 1993. The engine was one of fifty-five constructed in two batches to the designs of Robert Billinton by Vulcan Foundry – hence the unofficial class name of 'Vulcan's – between January 1893 and February 1902. No 445 left the Works in July 1894 and was provided with Marsh's larger 'C3' class boiler to become 'C2x' in March 1911, one of the forty-five so rebuilt. Withdrawal came in November 1961. ***RCR 6623***

Above: On 23rd June 1954 LMS Fowler '3MT' 2-6-2T No 40006 emerges into the sunlight at Crystal Palace with the 9.35am Willesden-East Croydon 'vans'. Until 1939 this was also a passenger service which, in its earlier LNWR days, also served the short-lived Croydon Central station. Perhaps it is worth noting the leading vehicle is of unmistakably Western origin though probably in carmine and cream rather than chocolate and cream. The service had ceased by the mid-1970s. *RCR 5140*

Opposite top: Billinton's 'E3' was the first of his four radial classes, coming into service from Brighton Works in October 1891. No 453 led the second batch of ten, entering traffic at New Cross [Gate] shed in April 1895 with the name *Broadbridge.* It is seen here on 13th November 1954 leading a long freight train out of Bricklayers Arms yard and past the imposing North Kent West Junction signal box with its frame of eighty levers. The engine's exhaust obscures the signals though the angle of the balance weights shows one has been cleared. As no headcode is displayed this is probably a signalled shunting movement. Despite the steady decline in freight traffic it was not until 1981 that the box and the branch were closed. No 32453 had long before surrendered to the cutter's torch, withdrawn from Bricklayers Arms shed only nine months after being captured by Dick's camera. *RCR 5639*

Opposite bottom: The valley of the River Effra is crossed by Bricklayers Arms-based 'C2x' class 0-6-0 No 32525 heading a Knights Hill sidings-Lillie Bridge freight. This view, dating from 1953, was captured from a position above the northern mouth of Knights Hill tunnel. The train consists, with one or two exceptions, of empty steel mineral wagons. Despite the rather nonchalant attitude of one crew member the 'distant' at 'caution' will have warned the driver Tulse Hill's home signal is at 'danger'. The engine was one of those in the second batch of the 'C2' class produced by Vulcan Foundry, coming into service in September 1900. Rebuilding to 'C2x' with a 'C3' class boiler occurred ten years later. No 32525 was among the last of its class to be withdrawn, in January 1962. *RCR 4523*

OXO

Opposite top: 'N1' class 'mogul' No 31876 was off for a pleasant day out in the country when Dick photographed it heading a down freight at St Mary Cray Junction on 8th May 1954. The line here is in the valley of the Kyd Brook, a tributary of the Ravensbourne which empties into the Thames at Deptford Creek; Petts Wood and the Hawkwood Estate rise beyond the train. The destination is not known but it may well be Faversham. The engine, allocated for much of its existence to Hither Green, left Ashford Works in March 1930 as A876, the first of the five production members of the class. The Holcroft conjugated gear to work the centre valve in the prototype, dating from March 1923, was not perpetuated, No A822 having already been reconstructed with three sets of Walschaerts gear. All six members of the class were withdrawn *en bloc* from Stewarts Lane in November 1962. *RCR 5107*

Opposite bottom: Bulleid 'utility''Q1' class 0-6-0 No 33009 approaches Factory Junction with a heavy Feltham-Hither Green freight, routed *via* Brentford. The 'Factory' is the former works of the LCDR, closed in 1911 when all its machinery and equipment and staff were transferred to Ashford; the junction the engine is about to make is with the low level lines from Stewarts Lane. The Chatham main line from Victoria, with the unmistakable bulk of Battersea Power Station forming a backdrop, sweeps in on the right. No 33009 left Brighton Works as No C9 in July 1942, one of twenty built there between March and December that year. Allocated new to Feltham, withdrawal of 33009 was from Nine Elms in September 1965. *RCR 10238*

This page: On 22nd September 1956 'N' class 2-6-0 No 31819 hustles its long train of vans from Maidstone East past St Mary Cray Junction signal box and along the spur to Chislehurst Junction *en route* to London Bridge. As the engine was allocated to Dover at this time it may well be some of the vans have come up from there. The connections between the main lines of the South Eastern and London, Chatham and Dover Railways at this point where they crossed were made in 1902 and 1904 following the 'Working Arrangement' of 1899. The engine was turned out of Ashford Works as No 819 in May 1922 and was among the last of the type withdrawn, in January 1964, from Guildford shed. *RCR 10016*

31852

Opposite: A heavy, mixed freight bound for the Chatham line heads south from Elmstead Woods in the charge of 'N' class 2-6-0 No 31852. The headcode could take the train right through to Dover *via* Ramsgate but I suspect it is heading for Faversham as at the time, 14th June 1958, the engine was allocated there. On the way however calls could be made at Rochester and Sittingbourne, perhaps also Gillingham. No 31852 was one of the fifty engines of the class ostensibly made at Woolwich though in reality the majority of those were assembled and finished at Ashford from parts manufactured at the Arsenal and boilers from outside suppliers. Nevertheless, the fact the Southern obtained them relatively cheaply earned the whole class the soubriquet 'Woolworths'. The eighty engines were scattered the whole length of the SR though rarer on the Central Section where the similar 'U' class predominated. They were particularly popular in the West Country with Exmouth Junction having anything up to thirty on the books though most were out-posted the length of the 'Withered Arm'. No 1852 left Ashford in March 1925 and had spells at Redhill as well as Faversham, returning to the Surrey crossroads following main line electrification in Kent, and being withdrawn from there in September 1963. Incidentally, note the telegraph wires are so numerous as to require double poles though all is nowadays at or below ground level. Note also the support under the fishplate joining the bull-head track on the line second from left. *RCR 12024*

Above: Another Maunsell 'N' class 2-6-0, this one No 31413 steams towards Longhedge Junction and the West London Line with an Inter-Regional freight on 27th February 1957. There are six parallel tracks here, the pair on the left curving in from Factory Junction on the ex-LCDR line, the other four from Stewarts Lane. These emanate from Victoria, Battersea Wharf, Battersea Power Station and the Great Western's South Lambeth goods depot. (Western 'panniers' shunting here in deepest Southern territory always seemed highly anachronistic.) Ahead is the viaduct carrying the ex-LBSCR main lines between Battersea Park and Clapham Junction opened in December 1867 to avoid the steep climb from Stewarts Lane to the bridge over the Thames; a connection from Longhedge Junction continues to be made with them at Pouparts Junction. The engine was the penultimate member of the eighty-strong class, entering traffic in January 1934 as part of a final batch of fifteen produced over twenty months from July 1932. Allocated to Stewarts Lane for much of its career, No 31413 was withdrawn from Guildford shed in July 1964. *RCR 8107*

7 Outer Suburbs

Above: British Railways 'Standard' class '4MT' No 75079 of Basingstoke shed powers along the down main at Durnsford Road heading for home with the 12.54pm from Waterloo, first stop Woking. The train is quite lengthy as this being a Saturday it has to carry all the half-day City workers from their offices. Designed at Brighton the first came into traffic in 1951; No 75079 was the final member of the class, constructed for the Southern Region at Swindon as part of the 1953 building programme. Another ten scheduled for 1954 for the Eastern Region were cancelled. The engine was withdrawn in November 1966. At present it is undergoing restoration at Ropley on the Mid-Hants Railway. *RCR 10284*

Opposite: Despite the scarred smokebox door indicative of past hard working, one of Wainwright's beautiful 'D' class 4-4-0s, No 31586, makes a spirited climb up the 1 in 83 from South Croydon to pass through Selsdon with the 5.40pm London Bridge to Tunbridge Wells West train *via* Hever. At this time it was a Tonbridge engine, having recently been reallocated from Faversham. The leading 3-car set No 954, dating from 1936, is also of interest, being part of the last order for 'steam' stock designed by Maunsell's Chief Carriage Draughtsman Lionel Lynes, though the style continued in the Portsmouth 4-CORs. There were, for example, frameless droplights, and on the corridor side doors were placed between alternate compartments rather than opposite every other one as in previous builds. No 954 was one of ten 3-coach sets turned out for the Western Section though they soon transferred to the Eastern. The set was disbanded in June 1959 and all three coaches had been withdrawn by the end of 1963. No 31586, which left Ashford in February 1907 as No 586, was withdrawn in September 1955. But we are fortunate somebody in authority recognised the 'D' as a supreme example of early 20th century artistic craftsmanship and saved no 737 for the nation. One other item takes attention, the up starter signal on its tall, tapered timber post with lower quadrant co-acting arms, still in use more than thirty years after the Brighton company ceased to exist. *RCR 4304*

780

Above: East Croydon on 1st July 1950: 'H2' class 'Atlantic' No 32421, *South Foreland,* is evidently eager to get away to London Bridge on the last stage of its journey from Brighton, having called at Lewes and then all stations to Sanderstead *via* Sheffield Park and East Grinstead. Dick makes no mention of the time but as there were a very limited number of trains on weekdays over this route – others terminated at Victoria, East Grinstead or Oxted – it is possible from the picture to make an educated guess at it. The sun is not quite direct from the east and the shadow is of moderate length and degree which suggests this is the 8.00am from Brighton, due to call here at 10.22am. The 1st class saloon in the centre coach of this 'Birdcage' set was, from personal experience when I could get away with it, very comfortable, and its large windows gave ample opportunity to view the passing countryside. Note the LMS corridor vehicle standing at platform two, and look too above the rooftop of the station building where the appropriate signal is 'cleared' for that train to continue. 'Through' trains between companies north of the Thames and the South Coast had a long history. That train is on the down 'local' line later extended by the LBSCR to avoid Redhill but which, anachronistically, then carried main line services *via* the 'Quarry Line'. It means going back to the time the Brighton and South Eastern were ordered by Parliament to share the Brighton's route between Norwood and Redhill to learn exactly why this anachronism persisted. It was not finally eliminated until 1984 with the reconfiguring of Gloucester Road Junction as part of the Brighton Line resignalling scheme. No 421, named *South Foreland* in 1925, was the first of the 'H2' class into traffic, leaving Brighton Works in June 1911. At Grouping it was at Brighton but alternated with Newhaven, a regular posting for the class for use on the Newhaven Boat Trains. It was one of the four withdrawn in Summer 1956 after faults present in the leading bogie were deemed too expensive to repair in view of the limited remaining life of the engine. *RCR 4050*

Opposite top: A Brighton-built LMR Fairburn '4MT' 2-6-4T gathers speed up the 1 in 83 through Selsdon with the 6.10pm – 'The terrible 6.10' - from Victoria to Uckfield, next stop Oxted. This was a Brighton engine but a Stewarts Lane duty which Dick Hardy said was accomplished only 'with a moderate degree of success'. He also says it was an easier task if Brighton found an 'Atlantic' for the job. I have pleasant recollections of these lovely engines 'chirruping' through Clapham Junction on this turn with ten bogies, first stop East Croydon in seventeen minutes. (In later days it was not unusual to find Brighton instead sending up a 'Light Pacific' on the 1.55pm for this duty.) No 42087 has only six coaches behind it, two sets of three, Bulleid and Maunsell, because the rear four coaches brought down from Victoria were detached at East Croydon as shown in the next image.... . *RCR 6621*

This page bottom: Shortly after No 42087 had cleared the section ahead 'M7' class 0-4-4T No 30054 appeared with the 6.36pm from East Croydon 'all-stations' Sanderstead to Tunbridge Wells West *via* Hever, the rear part of the 6.10pm. It is due at TWW at 7.45pm. The train, in carmine and cream, appears to be a Bulleid 3-set with a 'loose' coach at the rear. The date is 30th August 1955 by which time the engine had been transferred from Fratton to Brighton. It had been built at Nine Elms in December 1905, one of five to order No B13, and was withdrawn from Brighton shed in January 1959. *RCR 6622*

Just what amalgamation was all about! A 'push-pull' set of ex-LSWR stock is propelled away from Upper Warlingham station by an ex-SECR 'H' class 0-4-4T No 31523 past a Southern Railway rail-built signal post with an SR upper quadrant signal. The line is a joint LBSCR/ SER enterprise, opened in 1884, the former company providing the signal box, the latter the station building. And a Westinghouse signal for the shunt movement. Beyond the photograph being located among others for June 1956 Dick Riley gives neither a date nor a time. However, I think this may be a Saturdays Excepted train leaving East Croydon for Tunbridge Wells West *via* Edenbridge Town at about 1.55pm. (On Saturdays it would have started at London Bridge.) It provided at that time a connection out of the 1.8pm from Victoria to the same destination but by way of East Grinstead. When I knew it in the early fifties the stock was a three-coach 'birdcage' set berthed in a siding near East Croydon's south box until a Fairburn 2-6-4T appeared soon after one, drew it back out of sight into the sidings between the station's platforms 2 and 3 and, having run round, reappeared to couple up to the set again and commune quietly with itself until the departure time approached. Unfortunately we rarely saw this happen for as soon as the 1.8pm went by it was on our bikes and back to school with all haste for afternoon registration.

The dull day does nothing to brighten the miserable look of a once splendid engine very near the end of its usefulness. Earle Marsh had produced a poor 4-4-2T engine in the form of the class 'I1' and an even poorer one in the 'I2' but fortunately the 'I3' was in a class of its own. Perhaps some of the credit ought to go to others. The first in the class, No 21, which left Brighton Works in October 1907, was a tank engine version of Robert Billinton's fine 'B4' class 4-4-0. But the first production engine, No 22, did not appear for another two years. This was still essentially the 'B4' but with some significant detail alterations and, most significantly, a superheater. Marsh met Wilhelm Schmitt while visiting Germany and had been shown the superheater he had invented. But it is believed Marsh's Chief Draughtsman, Basil Field, was responsible for persuading Marsh to install it. Another year passed before four more of the class, Nos 23-26, entered traffic. Marsh, however, appears not to have been entirely convinced, for six saturated engines were produced between May 1909 and March 1910 for comparative purposes. The pictured No 75 was one of these. The running of the 'Sunny South Express' showed the superiority of the superheated engines when, in 1909 and at the instigation of the London & North Western Railway, engine changing took place at Rugby rather than Willesden. Having taken water at East Croydon, No 23 consistently proved capable of running the ninety miles to Rugby without needing more and to make the return Brighton-Rugby-Brighton round trip on a single bunker of coal, about 3¼ tons. The North Western, always proud to show off its engines, had nothing to match this. The fifteen 'I3's produced between October 1910 and March 1913 were all equipped with superheaters from new and the six saturated engines were retro-fitted by the Southern, No 75 in November 1925. The picture is undated but No 32075, seen approaching Norwood Junction with a train from Redhill that probably started from Tonbridge, must be only months away from withdrawal, in October 1951. ***RCR 4323***

34089
39

Opposite top: A down 'Continental' passes Bromley South under the charge of 'Battle of Britain' 4-6-2 No 34089, *602 Squadron,* on 25th May 1958. The leading vehicle is a Maunsell 'Nondescript' brake, possibly labelled or boarded for 2nd class travel and dating from the earliest years of the Southern Railway. The goods yard seen on the left was quite restricted in size and did no more than augment the far larger yard at Bromley North, while the siding to the right led to the local gasworks about ½-mile away. Under the Kent Coast Electrification scheme the line on which the train is travelling became the Up Chatham Slow. *RCR 11842*

Opposite Bottom: The cleared 'splitting distant' confirms the No 17 headcode. This train is for Ramsgate and will bear left at the end of the platform at Chislehurst to take the spur to St Mary Cray Junction and the ex-LCDR line to the coast. The date is 22nd September 1956, a Saturday at a time when half-day working in the City was then still customary. The long rake of Bulleid coaches in Carmine and Cream with 'BB' class 'pacific' No 34075, *264 Squadron*, at its head suggests this may well be either the 'Saturdays Only' 12.45pm or 1.15pm from Cannon Street, fast to Chatham in forty-six minutes. Both included a Refreshment Car to satiate the thirst of exhausted City workers. The sidings on the left lead to the goods yard, the site of the temporary terminus titled Chislehurst & Bickley Park when the 'new' SER line to Tonbridge *via* Orpington and Sevenoaks opened this far from St Johns on 1st July 1865. When pictured No 34075 was a Dover engine but transfer to Exmouth Junction followed completion of the Kent Coast Electrification Scheme; withdrawal from that shed was in April 1964. *RCR 10006*

Above: A down 'Continental' has diverged from the Chatham main line at Bickley Junction and drifts along the 1902 loop to join the ex-SER line from London Bridge at Petts Wood Junction. The signal box is very typical of the Chatham with its sliding sash windows though note that the windows in the locking room have been bricked up as a wartime safety measure. The engine is No 34087, *145 Squadron. RCR 12233*

Above: On 1st August 1954 'Schools' class 4-4-0 No 30932, *Blundells*, heading a train for Dover, passes through Knockholt station with the end of the eleven-mile climb from St Johns in sight. The station – which appears to be undergoing a facelift - was opened as 'Halstead for Knockholt' on 1st May 1876, eight years after the line. It is, however, fairly remote from both villages, Knockholt being about a mile distant and Halstead further still. Chalk was harvested from the cliff face on the down side to rebuild the trackbed and sea defences at Reculvers after the devastating floods along the Thames Estuary in February 1953. Incidentally, the tender coupled to *Blundells* was reconstructed in 1938 with high sides turned in to match the cab profile though the engine did not have a monopoly of this tender. A long-time resident of Bricklayers Arms shed, No 30932 was withdrawn from Ashford in January 1961. *RCR 5207*

Opposite top: One can almost hear and feel the roar of 'L1' class No 31784 as it tops the 1 in 95 climb from Bromley South, for as a body the Wainwright/Maunsell inside-cylinder 4-4-0s could raise a decibel level even a 'King Arthur' 'on song' could not sustain. As one fireman recounts, his driver's advice on when to fire on his first boarding an 'L1' was "don't listen to her, watch the chimney". Here the engine is passing the galaxy of signals worked by the distant Bickley Junction box as it heads east on the 'down fast'. This is Tuesday 14th August 1954, the Summer timetable will be coming to an end the following month and the intense holiday traffic is dwindling away. Like its fourteen classmates No 31784 was built by North British (Works No 2365) and delivered in April 1926 as A784. After many years allocated to Bricklayers Arms, and made redundant following the first stage of the Kent Coast electrification in 1959, withdrawal from Nine Elms came in February 1960. *RCR 5219*

Opposite bottom: Out and about on 11th May 1954, Dick captured an unidentified 'light pacific' leading a Ramsgate *via* Chatham train towards Chislehurst tunnel. This is the earlier of the two tunnels, dating from 1865, the other from quadrupling of the line, though in driving it the original was damaged and had to be closed for nearly four months while repairs were undertaken. The line reopened on 3rd November 1903. The survey had called for a cutting here but the landowner refused access. As a result parts of the overlying land are no more than four feet above the tunnels' arches. The train is on the 'slow' line, the tunnel being 649 yards long in contrast to the new, 'fast' line tunnel at 591 yards. Elmstead Woods station, which lies immediately south of the tunnels, opened with the completion of quadrupling in July 1904 though the tunnels still bear the name 'Chislehurst'. *RCR 5118*

31506

Opposite top: 'E1' class 4-4-0 No 31506 gets to grips with the 1 in 95 from Bromley South heading an excursion for Sheerness on 25th May 1958. The sands are working to aid departure and the blasting exhaust can be heard all over town. It looks as though the Stirllng steam reverser is in operation which assumes the driver is already notching up, the safety valves are humming so the 'Kentish dust' on the tender is just what 31506 likes, and everything appears to be in fine fettle. Perhaps it is all an illusion, for four months later the engine left Stewarts Lane for the last time. *RCR 11846*

Opposite bottom: A carelessly placed reporting number clothes this 'BB' class 'pacific' in anonymity as it reaches the top of the 1 in 100/95 climb from Shortlands at Bickley Junction. From the state of the exhaust and the early hint of steam from the safety valves it is likely the train called at Bromley South and the engine was required to exert considerable power to get it moving again up that sharp gradient. No doubt at least one injector will be on to keep the boiler quiet in the dive down into the Cray valley as well as to raise the water level. The date is Saturday 24th July 1954, the start of the busiest part of the summer timetable that came into effect six weeks earlier. Trains for the North Kent Coast will begin to be identified by their reporting number to aid signalmen dealing particularly with intense Saturday traffic. This particular service is for Ramsgate and appears to consist of Maunsell stock in green though the last two vehicles would appear to have acquired carmine and cream. Note the fourth rail here. The dull surface confirms it is not touched by any shoes, its function being to improve the return part of the power circuit otherwise carried by the running rails. Note too the signalman seated in the window but looking to the east, ready to check the train has its requisite tail lamp. *RCR 5199*

Above: On 14th October 1958 BR class '5MT' 4-6-0 No 73082 begins its 1 in 100 run down into the Cray valley from St Mary Cray Junction. Having climbed out of the London Basin this is the fourth valley the engine will have challenged in the fifteen miles from Victoria as it has also already crossed those of the Beck at Beckenham and the Ravensbourne at Bromley. It will face a much longer fall and rise to cross the Darent at Farningham Road and the deeper still Medway valley at Rochester. It is thus easy to understand that when the South Eastern and the Chatham came to their working agreement in 1899, junctions were soon put in where the two routes crossed one another nearby to enable the main Continental traffic from Victoria to be routed over the easier SER line to the Channel ports. On transfer to Nine Elms and withdrawal of the appropriate 'N15' No 73082 acquired the name *Tintagel* in 1959. *RCR 12022*

Opposite: A photo from 14th June 1958 shows sister 5MT No 73080 bringing a train along the curving spur line between Bickley Junction and Petts Wood Junction. The 'Loop' was opened on 8th September 1902, the corresponding Up loop six days later. The two loops between Chislehurst and St Mary Cray followed in June 1904. The scene here was originally titled Orpington Junction as Petts Wood station did not open until July 1928. As the leading vehicle is a Continental Nondescript brake, the headcode is for a train to Dover or Folkestone and the smokebox carries a board with a reporting number, it is safe to assume this is a Boat Train for one of the Channel ports. Though design work was done at Doncaster, construction of the 5MT class was mainly carried out at Derby. This engine was the first of a batch of ten built there for the Southern Region in 1954; in 1959 it was named *Merlin. RCR 12014*

Above: This photograph dates from 16th May 1959 when many works in connection with the Kent Coast electrification had been completed. These included improving existing track infrastructure to increase speed and capacity. 'BB' class 'pacific' No 34085, *501 Squadron,* takes full advantage as it brings the "Golden Arrow" Boat train towards Petts Wood on the straightened spur from Bickley Junction. Everything is still raw so the original curving approach can be discerned above the train. Note also that a direct connection is made to the down fast line whereas a crossover had previously been provided for this move; the signal arm now missing from the 'doll' confirms it has gone. Note too that by this time ordinary coaches had become commonplace among the First-class 'Pullmans'. The train first ran in May 1929 though the Nord company had introduced the equivalent "Fleche d'Or" service between Calais and Paris in 1926. Ordinary carriages were introduced among the Pullmans in 1931, a direct consequence of the economic downturn of that period, and the train naturally ceased to run during the war years. It was re-introduced as an 'All-Pullman' service in April 1946 although as before that did not last. Despite some asserting to the contrary the 'Golden Arrow' never crossed the Channel; only the 'Night Ferry' went to sea. Demand for this style of rail travel declined in the 1960s though my wife and I took advantage of the 1st class on offer and travelled in Pullman comfort when going to Paris on honeymoon in 1964, albeit a Sunday diversion *via* the Catford loop and Maidstone East. "The Arrer" last ran on 30th September 1972. *RCR 13328*

Above: On Saturday 22nd September 1956 'L1'class 4-4-0 No 31758 gathers speed down the 1 in 146 towards Elmstead Woods with a train for Charing Cross. This has come up from Dover *via* Maidstone East and the St Mary Cray Junction-Chislehurst Junction spur. The Southern signal post guarding the Down main line, made of two used bullhead rails bolted together, supports Chislehurst's Home and Chislehurst Junction's slotted Distant signals worked by the box on the right alongside the goods yard's headshunt. It would be another two and a half years before the semaphores were taken down, the post uprooted and both boxes closed, and colour-lights worked from the new Chislehurst Junction box, appropriately sited in the middle of the confusion of lines, came into operation. Goods facilities were withdrawn in November 1986 but two sidings were retained for some years for ARC mineral traffic. No 31758 had come into service from North British (Works No 23361) in March 1926, working out of Bricklayers Arms shed before a move in the late 1950s to Ashford. As with the whole of its class the onset of the Kent Coast Electrification scheme saw the engine posted to Nine Elms from which shed it was withdrawn in October 1959. *RCR 10008*

8 Interlopers

Opposite bottom: 'Schools' class No 30924, *Haileybury,* brings its tidy rake of ex-SECR 'Birdcage' stock forming the 2.36pm(SO) Charing Cross-Hastings service past the entrance to Chislehurst goods yard on 14th August 1954. One fireman wrote that the large chimneyed 'Schools' – No 30924 was one of the twenty-one fitted with this and a multiple-jet blastpipe by Bulleid - needed careful firing, for pressure would 'hang' if the fire was blacked out under the door, not a failing with those in original small-chimney condition. *Haileybury* was the last of a batch of ten built at Eastleigh in 1933, into service in December and acquired its large chimney in September 1940. The engine spent much of its early service at Dover but by this time was at Bricklayers Arms. It ended its career at Redhill and it would be comforting to know it had a few final trips along that scenically beautiful line beneath the Downs to Guildford prior to withdrawal in January 1962. It may be worth noting that before Michael Heseltine decided to bring the Hi-Speed link from the Channel Tunnel around East London, the large houses in the background were 'blighted' for many months by proposals to take it at least partway alongside the existing SER route by widening the embankment to accommodate it. Much more than the back garden would have been lost. *RCR 5212*

Above: On 24th April 1953 the crank axle of Merchant Navy class No 35020, *Bibby Line*, fractured at speed at Crewkerne. Later that year the entire class was temporarily withdrawn for the axles to be tested, Nine Elms borrowing 'Black 5's and 'V2's to cover the shortfall. In this undated view, probably late August or September 1953, Dick captured 'V2' No 60908 at Vauxhall with a train for Southampton Terminus, or so the headcode implies. Such passenger trains appear very rarely in the timetable so it is certain this – a five-coach Bulleid set in carmine and cream livery followed by what appears to be an early Maunsell vehicle still in green with a van bringing up the rear – is instead one of the regular xx54 minutes past the hour semi-fast services to Basingstoke. *RCR 4531*

Top: The London & North Western, the Midland and the Great Northern all had goods depots or coal yards on Southern territory in London, the latter two companies as rewards for their financial assistance to the London, Chatham & Dover Railway for its Metropolitan Extension. But here we see Gresley 'J50/4' class 0-6-0T No 68979 hurrying past Peckham Rye shops not with coal but instead a mixed Hornsey-Hither Green freight on 28th February 1957. The route epitomises the difficulties faced by such cross-London traffic with its sharp curves and steep gradients at, for example, Snow Hill – where a banker is provided – Loughborough Junction and Parks Bridge Junction (Lewisham), where neither of these will have one. It is noticeable that while passenger engines traversing the Widened Lines were instructed to 'Condense', the J50s which regularly passed along that same section of track were never fitted with condensers. *RCR 10249*

Bottom: 'Foreigners' at rest at Norwood shed on 15th September 1963. Built as a Drummond 'T9', 4-4-0 No 120 and almost-Drummond Caledonian 'single' No 123 worked two legs of the 'Scottish Belle' railtour that day between Victoria and Haywards Heath. The 'single' was constructed in 1886 by Neilsons of Glasgow as an exhibition engine, and in conjunction with the Caledonian built a larger version of Drummond's '66' class 4-4-0 to go with it. Both were awarded Gold Medals and both went to the Caledonian afterwards. Meanwhile 'T9' No 120 was the eighth member of the class to appear from Nine Elms, in August 1899. By 1923 five engines of the class had been fitted with a superheater in a higher-pitched boiler and an associated extended smokebox on a saddle, the Southern so treating the rest, No 120 dealt with in May 1927. Neither engine pictured appears here in 'as built' condition which begs the question of accuracy of their pre-Grouping livery. Perhaps generosity ought to overcome pedanticism and we should just be grateful both have been preserved. *RCR 17338*

Top: Stanier '8F' 2-8-0 No 48410 raises the echoes in the retaining walls at Denmark Hill as it passes with a freight for Hither Green. It is probable the headcode is No 9 which, in Cross-London terms, means the train emanated from Brent Sidings at Cricklewood and took the roundabout route to the Windsor side of Clapham Junction through Acton Wells and Kew East Junction. The ex-LCDR line on which the train is now travelling would have been reached at Factory Junction. No fewer than 130 engines of this 852-strong class were built in four 'lots' at the three Southern Railway workshops in 1943-4 although Swindon turned out No 8410. The SR's Orders came from the Railway Executive, other than twenty-five turned out from Brighton in 1944 for the LNER which classified them as 'O6'. *RCR 6002*

Bottom: While Nine Elms got 'V2's and 'Black 5's as substitutes for its lost 'pacifics' after No 35020 broke its crank axle, Stewarts Lane acquired Thompson 'B1' 4-6-0s, hence the appearance of No 61329 at Herne Hill on Tuesday 22nd September. The train is bound for Ramsgate though Dick makes no note of the time, neither does the dull weather permit of a hazardous guess at it. According to Richard Hardy, the Doncaster-trained Shedmaster at Stewarts Lane, the crews were generally appreciative of these engines after a trip or two though the ride quality could be rough at times when compared to that of a Bulleid 'pacific'. *RCR 4575*

Left: From the rather casual attitude of the driver class 'J50/4' No 68989 has things well in hand as it climbs with a freight train from Stewarts Lane to Factory Junction on 27th February 1957. No headcode discs but the single lamp above the nearside buffer is for Cross-London route No 3, signifying in this instance 'Eastern Region and Battersea Yard *via* Blackfriars'. Clearly what happens thereafter, north of the latter, is of no interest to Southern signalmen though having passed through the Widened Lines and under King's Cross the ultimate destination is Hornsey. ***RCR 8109***

Bottom: Although Great Western 'panniers' had held sway for years in the company's South Lambeth goods depot the sight of one on the South Western main line could be a new and rather disturbing experience. With the 'M7's that had long dominated empty workings between Waterloo and Clapham Junction feeling their age, surplus members of the '5700' class were allocated to Nine Elms to relieve them. Less than a year before Dick took this photo on 20th June 1959 No 4634, seen at Vauxhall heading empty stock into Waterloo, had been working out of Cardiff (Cathays) shed. ***RCR 13686***

Right: Brixton station sees LNER class 'J50/4' 0-6-0T No 68979 come off the Catford Loop on 28th February 1957 with freight, doubtless from Hornsey where the engine is allocated. The cleared 'Distant' signal shows that at Shepherds Lane Junction, a quarter-mile further on, it will be moved over to the up line leading directly to Factory Junction. In the absence of a headcode the destination cannot be noted with certainty but Stewarts Lane is the leading probability. However, the Windsor side of Clapham Junction and a direct run to Feltham are equally quite possible.
RCR 10279

Bottom; Maunsell 'W' class 2-6-4T No 31916 finds itself hemmed in on home ground at Hither Green by an unidentified 'J50/4' 0-6-0T and former Great Eastern 'J19' 0-6-0 No 64664 when Dick visited on 21st February 1960. The latter engine, allocated to Stratford, was one of two in the class provided with smaller cylinders but higher pressure than the other twenty-five. It had likely brought in a freight from Temple Mills, almost circumnavigating London by travelling over the Tottenham & Hampstead Junction Joint line to Gospel Oak and then to the West London Line *via* Kensal Rise and Mitre Bridge Junction. Leaving the WLL at Latchmere Main Junction brought it to Factory Junction and the Chatham main line. Thereafter it took the Catford Loop to Nunhead, the part of the ex-LCDR Greenwich Park branch refurbished in 1929 and the new causeway and loop of that same year, to bring it to the ex-SER main line at Parks Bridge Junction, Lewisham. *RCR 14464*

Above: Grimy Neasden allocated 'Black 5' No 44830 brings what Dick describes as a 'City of Leicester Holiday Express' into Tulse Hill on Monday 10th August 1959. The engine is showing the BR standard 'A' headcode for an 'express passenger, newspaper, or breakdown train' and so on. Maybe the crew discouraged the Southern pilotman from interfering to change it to a unique SR route code. But maybe not. This has to be the return working because the train has come in from the south and the line it is on only provides access to the 1869 ex-LCDR spur to Herne Hill. In that respect it is just possible the headcode may be correct for it signifies among others 'Victoria or Battersea Yard and Portsmouth *via* Thornton Heath, West Croydon and Horsham'. The obvious continuation of such a route for traffic to the north would be through Clapham Junction and the West London Railway but that would not provide a direct link to the former Great Central line. If this surmising is right, the service has started from somewhere on or near the Hampshire coast and is routed this way so as to gain the Windsor side of Clapham Junction and travel on through New and East Junctions at Kew to meet the former GC line at Neasden Junction. One thing we do know for sure is that Tulse Hill's uncompromisingly solid signalbox dates from 1945, its predecessor having been bombed to destruction. *RCR 14078*

Opposite top: Work is going on at London Bridge on 29th April 1954 as the two Bulleid 'double-deck' sets forming the 4.23pm from Gravesend to Charing Cross arrive alongside platform 4. Platform lengthening for the 10-car scheme is already well advanced and the No 5 road once running between the two in view has long been lifted to allow for it. The Greenwich line viaduct stretches away into the murk while the massive water tank and the signal box, one of the three opened here on 7th June 1928, are set in the sea of tracks between the terminal and 'through' parts of the station. The box had a frame of 311 levers that controlled 216 signal functions and 79 points. The two 'DD' units were in reality more 1½-deck with alternate upper and lower sets of seats, never popular with the travelling public nor, come to that, with the operators, the longstanding 20-second halt at suburban stations being difficult to maintain because of the potentially larger number of passengers at each door compared with normal stock. They were withdrawn without regret on 1st October 1971 though two motor coaches are believed to survive in private ownership. *RCR 5090*

9 Panoramas

Bottom: Hungerford bridge, photographed on a typically dull December day in 1958, came into use when the line from London Bridge opened to Charing Cross station on 11th January 1864. The Brunel-designed Hungerford Suspension bridge had opened on 1st May 1845 to give pedestrian access from the South bank to the Hungerford market on the north shore of the Thames but the tolls received were insufficient to make it financially successful. Its removal followed authorisation of the Charing Cross Railway in 1859. (The pedestrian footpath the railway was obliged to continue may just be made out through the down side girders.) The railway bridge was designed by John Hawkshaw who made use of the foundations of the brick towers that had supported the suspension chains; those were later sold for use in the Clifton Suspension Bridge. The 1826 shot tower and the Royal Festival Hall, all that remains on the 1951 Festival site, dominate the south bank to the east while the gabled roofs of Waterloo station can be seen to the west. However, the cranes show London is rebuilding and the view will have changed dramatically within a few years. Having been 'released' is the Bulleid 'light pacific' backing out of the station on to the adjacent down line to head for Ewer Street or 'The Brick'? Or is it slowly coming in to buffer up to empty stock and release a fellow? The siding on the left-hand part of the bridge is, like the engine, no longer, permitting much lengthened platforms to be installed and the approach pointwork simplified. ***RCR 12982***

Top: Stewarts Lane depot photographed from a train passing on the main LCDR line presents the smoky murk endemic in the atmosphere above such an installation. An 'H' class 0-4-4T is replenishing its tanks while a 'P' class 0-6-0T keeps the coal wagons in their place. But most noticeable among the resting engines is an Eastern Region 'B1'class 4-6-0, one of those borrowed when the 'Merchant Navy' class engines were temporarily withdrawn. *RCR 4585*

Bottom: 'Battle of Britain' No 34071, *601 Squadron,* is at Factory Junction on the last lap of its journey from Dover with a Boat train on Sunday 19th September 1954. It has come up over the difficult secondary route through Maidstone East and Swanley. The train appears to be entirely in carmine and cream livery, including the nondescript Brake that follows the two GUVs behind the engine. No 34071 was the first 'BB' to be completed at Brighton after nationalisation, part of order No 3383, and thus the first of its class not to have the '21C1' prefix to its number. It left the Works in April 1948. Rebuilding to the more conventional look under the auspices of R G Jarvis saw its reappearance into traffic in May 1960. Though Stewarts Lane cared for it for some years, it was shedded at Dover at the end of the 1950s but ended at Eastleigh as many engines did towards the end of steam, and was withdrawn from there in July 1967. On the right the South London Line sweeps away towards Battersea Park, a section abandoned since TfL's London Overground worked here from Peckham Rye and instead took 'The Ludgate Line' to Longhedge Junction and the north side of Clapham Junction. 'Abandoned' is, in fact, not quite true because Battersea Park sees a single London Overground arrival and departure on weekdays at each end of the day, Saturdays excepted. *RCR 5521*

Top: Are there actually sleepers beneath that deep layer of coal dust and ash hiding the sidings in Stewarts Lane depot? And how unusual is it to find two ex-LSWR engines together in this former SECR stronghold? A'700' class 0-6-0 sits alone in the sea of track while 'T9' No 30338 is beckoned forward by the 'shunt' signal on the bracket as it brings in a transfer freight from Nine Elms. This 'T9' was the last of fifteen of the class turned out by Nine Elms between December 1900 and October 1901. In these engines the splashers and cabs were to the full width of the footplate, suppressing the small splashers needed to cover the throw of the coupling rods as in earlier examples. As part of the fitment of superheaters, Urie substituted a stovepipe for Drummond's heavily-flared chimney. No 338 was one of the early SR conversions, in January 1923, which suggests it was in process before grouping. About a quarter of the sixty-six engines in the class were equipped to burn oil in 1947 under the Government-sponsored scheme though this did not last as the rising price of oil made it uneconomic. They were all laid aside in 1948 and never worked again, being officially withdrawn in 1951. When photographed on 27th February 1957 No 30338 was allocated to Nine Elms but transfer to the West Country followed shortly. Exmouth Junction was its last home, until April 1961. *RCR 10227*

Right: 'The Golden Arrow', 12.30pm departure from Paris Gare du Nord, and 5.23pm from Dover – always provided the Channel behaved itself - drifts down the Petts Wood Junction-Bickley Junction spur on Saturday 24th July 1954. The engine is the 'Festival of Britain' 'Britannia', No 70004, William Shakespeare, whose special exhibition finish was improved and maintained by Stewarts Lane's '6.0am' cleaners. But as Shedmaster Dick Hardy commented 'she could come back home covered in dirt and mud from end to end'. Perhaps that is a reminder that in the seventy-eight miles to Dover the train passed through ten tunnels with a total length of almost eight miles, in other words about 10% of the journey was spent underground. Incidentally, the local railwayman's runner beans seem to be doing well. *RCR 5201*

Top: The London skyline at the end of the 1950s presents a very different view to that nowadays. Quite apart from the complete rebuilding of London Bridge station early in the 21st century, St Paul's is no longer the dominant feature, neither do the cranes wave their heads above the roofs of the warehouses used now for smart offices or even smarter residential accommodation compared with storing the masses of produce imported from around the world. The train led by the 2-HAP unit will follow the river closely as far as Gravesend before turning inland to the Medway at Strood and the terminus at Gillingham. The full Kent Coast service beyond that outer suburban point was instituted on 14th June 1959, exactly one month after Dick took this picture. One point of note is the then-rare freight train visible alongside platform 4, heading for Blackfriars and Snow Hill tunnel and that foreign territory north of the Thames. ***RCR 13299***

Bottom: Cannon Street and its bridge across the Thames on Wednesday 29th April 1955. It's a pity Dick gives no indication of the time but I suspect this is towards the end of the morning rush hour as he states this is empty stock on its way out. The engines are identified as 'C2x' No 32553, of Bricklayers Arms, and '2MT' 2-6-2T No 41292 of Stewarts Lane, which merely adds to the mix. Were they heading directly down through London Bridge to Rotherhithe Road sidings, or maybe going further, to Maze Hill or Blackheath? Or, because there are two engines, perhaps as an aid with shunting movements, is the stock maybe going in the opposite direction, through Metropolitan Junction towards Blackfriars and then reversing to head towards Stewarts Lane or out to the suburbs, again Maze Hill or Blackheath *via* Nunhead and Lewisham, even perhaps to the vast Eardley Sidings in Streatham? Charing Cross is obviously a possibility but with two engines and platforms of restricted length I think it unlikely. We shall never know now. ***RCR 5719***

10 Stations

The Brighton did not stint on stations set in the upmarket areas of its system. Dulwich was most certainly one where the potential clientele needed to be impressed. This is North Dulwich, on the line from Sutton to Peckham Rye, opened on 1st October 1868 and, as the name implies, on the northern fringe of the village. It is still there though the magnificent chimneys and decorative balustrade about the two-storey part have gone as has the intrusive sign over the centre arch. The windows and fascias of the shops are rather more discreet nowadays too. The basic structure of the building is in red brick. *RCR 4436*

This was the station building at Mitcham until the West Croydon-Wimbledon line closed at the end of May 1997 for the route to be taken into the Croydon Tramlink system. The listed building, in yellow- grey brick, dates from the turn of the 18th century and is commonly claimed to have been the headquarters of the Surrey Iron Railway which opened on 26th July 1803. There is, however, no definite evidence to substantiate the claim. 'Station Court', formerly a merchant's house, has returned to being a residential property. *RCR 5682*

Top: Dilapidation Rules! This is Upper Sydenham station with a Bulleid 4-SUB on a Blackfriars-Crystal Palace (HL) working leaving the 400-yard-long Upper Sydenham tunnel. The line from Peckham Rye was opened by the Crystal Palace & South London Railway on 1st August 1865 though worked by the Chatham from the first. The CP&SLJR was a very independently–minded concern with ambitions to extend to the Brighton near Brockley and the South Eastern at Lewisham. The Chatham would not tolerate such ambition and went to Court to prevent it, claiming it had always run the line at a loss and having already threatened to bankrupt the small company by running trains into the Brighton's Crystal Palace station instead. To that end it had raised a tightly-curved embankment – still visible - between its main line west of Beckenham Junction and the part of the Crystal Palace & West End of London line east of Bromley Junction it had leased in 1863 and later purchased. Track was laid but never provided a 'through' connection. Having lost the case the CP&SLJR sank reluctantly into LCDR ownership. Upper Sydenham station itself did not open until 1st August 1884 and, like the rest of the branch, closed between January 1917 and March 1919 and again from mid-1944 to March 1946. Although traffic had been diminishing the fire that destroyed the Crystal Palace on the night of 30th November 1936 effectively sealed the branch's fate. Renewal of power cabling which had been in place since electrification in July 1925 could not be justified in view of the sparse traffic. The line closed on 20th September 1954. *RCR 4832*

Bottom: Brixton station looking west as a South London Line train bound for Victoria enters the heavy girders of the Atlantic Road viaduct. (This was reconstructed in 1989 to carry heavy Continental freight traffic.) The station opened on 25th August 1862 with the first part of the LCDR's independent line between the capital and Beckenham though the platforms on the Catford Loop here were taken out of use around 1929. The train, a 2-car set of ex-Overhead SLL stock - note the dip in the roof where the pantograph was mounted – has just left East Brixton station with its timber buildings and platforms perched precariously on high piers alongside the approach viaduct. The last of the SLL sets went in September 1954 to be superseded by new 2-EPB sets but East Brixton, despite a falling away in traffic, lasted for some time longer. Extension of the Victoria line south to Brixton had a marked effect on its use and a fire in the station in 1975 may have been an excuse for its closure. It was however reopened but the prohibitive cost of a full renovation could not be justified. Closure came on 5th January 1976. But Brixton station itself continues to attract custom, more than 1.2 million passengers passing through in the year 2018-9. *RCR 4840*

Top: Charing Cross on Wednesday 3rd December 1958, with EPB stock occupying three of the six platforms. Dick makes no note of the time of day but would it be too far-fetched to suppose the Bulleid 'light pacific' gearing itself up to depart tender first from platform six may be taking now-empty stock round the corner from Metropolitan Junction to form a peak-hour service from Cannon Street? The Charing Cross hotel was the regular meeting point for the Southern Board to hold its discussions and remains open for business though the rest of the station has undergone wholesale reconstruction. But the insignia are still there. ***RCR 12983***

Bottom: Not quite 'the walls came tumbling down' but Cannon Street is a sad sight as the final part of its roof is demolished in January 1959. It does, however, indicate just what problems the Southern and the other companies – and the Nationalised railways that followed them - faced in London and other major cities after the war. The short canopies along the platforms were erected when almost all the glass was lost in that period. The station opened on 1st September 1866 with the branch from the Charing Cross Railway at Borough Market Junction. Its platforms have always outnumbered those of its West End counterpart, an indication of the greater perceived importance of the City. The method of working until the early years of the 20th century confirms this, all trains being worked into Cannon Street and only a proportion then reversing to go out through Metropolitan Junction to Waterloo Junction and Charing Cross. That method has had an effect to this day as there are still only two lines between Borough Market Junction and Metropolitan Junction for direct Charing Cross traffic because this part of the triangle was intended only for light engine and ECS movements. Though the 'in-and-out' system of working had largely ceased by the turn of the 19th century, it took preparations for electrification at the beginning of 1926 to make wholesale and rational changes to the station's approach layout to take account of it. A commercial building now spans the whole station though the brick towers at the river end of the sidewalls that once supported the magnificent overall roof survive and are now listed. ***RCR 12995***

1803
2

WAY OUT

Opposite top: The unprepossessing Clapham station photographed on the dullest of days in October 1953. Titled Clapham & North Stockwell it opened with the first part of the LCDR's independent route from Victoria to Beckenham on 25th August 1862. But this is the Brighton part, with a South London Line former 'overhead' unit en route to London Bridge. It opened with the South London Line on 1st August 1865, the Chatham side of the station being sited to the right of shot. Towards the end of the 19th century it began to suffer from local tramway competition and while the Brighton arrested decline by electrifying the SLL in 1909 use of the Chatham side diminished and it closed in 1916 as a wartime economy measure, never to reopen. Parts of the right-wing media once dubbed Clapham 'the worst kept station in London'. It would have been kinder to label it 'the most abused'. Nowadays the station is in the care of London Overground and neither Victoria nor London Bridge is now directly accessible from it. ***RCR 4839***

Opposite bottom: Elmers End station opened on 1st April 1864 with the southward extension of the Mid-Kent Railway from Beckenham to Addiscombe Road, the line being leased by the SER. The brick station building with its arched canopy over the platform is very typical of South Eastern stations constructed over the last forty years of the 19th century and persisted into the 20th as evidenced by those at Elmstead Woods, Chislehurst and Orpington rebuilt at the quadrupling of the SER main line from St Johns between 1902 and 1904. The station suffered some damage during World War Two but it was not rebuilt until destroyed by fire in December 1973. A rather brutal glass and steel box now greets passengers. The train is a Hayes-Charing Cross working *via* the Ladywell Loop which avoids Lewisham. Numerically, the route became No 34 in EPB days. ***RCR 5202***

Above: Eden Park opened with the line from Elmers End to Hayes on 29th May 1882. It had been promoted by the West Wickham & Hayes Railway Company in 1880 and acquired by the South Eastern the following year. There was almost no development here until the railway came and not that much before electrification in February 1926. But in the eight years that followed ordinary ticket sales went up about nine-fold and more tellingly perhaps 'seasons' increased by almost fifteen times. The timber up side station building was damaged by fire but reroofed and provided with a new canopy as part of the electrification programme. The down platform was lengthened. Note the fourth rail, an aide to the return current. The branch is fed by the sub-station at Elmers End, 3¼ miles from Hayes and thus at about the limit of its effectiveness in powering the two 4-SUB units that comprise the train, Charing Cross to Hayes *via* Lewisham. ***RCR 5206***

S 5124
3
WAY OUT
SOUTHERN RAILWAY
LONDON
BOOKING OFFICE
18
WHYTE

Opposite top: The Shortlands & Nunhead Railway had been a long time in gestation, sanctioned after more than five years in process in August 1889, local landowners having become involved after previous attempts had failed. The line opened on 1st July 1892, worked by the Chatham which purchased it in 1896. James Staats Forbes, the Chatham's rogue of a Chairman and General Manager, contended he had long held a fear Penge tunnel would collapse so an alternative route avoiding it was a great advantage. Whether he had expressed that view before the S&DR was proposed is in doubt, but the fear did not prompt him or the Chatham to support the scheme other than verbally. Albemarle Cator, the owner of Beckenham Place, was among the proponents of the scheme and we see 'V' class 4-4-0 No 30938, *St Olave's*, photographed heading east with empty stock through his local station, Beckenham Hill, on 9th May 1959. Cator's presence here resulted in Beckenham Hill's building being unique among the line's stations, the only one in brick; all the others were of timber construction. The covered footbridge was typical though the original platform canopies have been superseded by standard SR ones. *RCR 13263*

Opposite bottom: Whyteleafe South station opened as Warlingham on 5th August 1856 with the Caterham Valley Railway's line from Purley. Warlingham itself lies only a ½-mile or so to the east but some 200 metres higher than the station set in the deep Caterham valley. The name was changed a few weeks short of a century later, on 11th June 1956. Being a South Eastern line the service in Southern days continued to be worked from Charing Cross and Cannon Street. However, not long after electrification of the ex-South Eastern suburban lines through London Bridge in 1926 and the resulting increase in traffic, capacity constraints meant branch rush-hour services could no longer work into the traditional termini. Herbert Walker wrote personally to all season ticket holders to explain the reasons for the change of terminus to London Bridge although there was still an outcry from those affected. A 4-EPB unit was working a Caterham-Purley shuttle service when Dick Riley photographed it on 6th August 1956. It is ironic that when the Oxted line opened from South Croydon in March 1884 the local station was named Upper Warlingham to provide a distinction. It remains so though there is no 'Lower' Warlingham in existence now. *RCR 6942*

Bottom: The new St Mary Cray station on 2nd May 1959 sees a train for Holborn Viaduct *via* the Catford Loop arriving. The five miles of track between Bickley Junction and Swanley were quadrupled as part of Phase 1 of the Kent Coast Electrification Scheme, requiring removal of more than a million tons of sand and clay and erection of ½-mile of concrete retaining walls as well as doubling in width the nine arches of the viaduct across the Cray Valley. Although constructed eleven years after nationalisation much of the station is pure Southern from the concrete works at Exeter. The most modernistic of items on view are the fluorescent lights with the station name on the covers. Further west the use and nomenclature of the four tracks between Bickley and Shortlands have been changed. Once paired by direction, they are now paired by use; the line the train is on, despite it being a local service, is the up main as that is the side of the formation by which it will access the Catford Loop. Much later developments in conjunction with Eurostar travel saw a double-track flyunder in place at Shortlands eliminate the necessary conflicting movement at Swanley. Ironic though, because even as the finishing touches went into it, plans for transfer of the terminus from Waterloo to St Pancras were already far advanced. *RCR 13233*

Above: The driver of the Cannon Street to Gravesend train *via* Bexleyheath getting smartly away from platform 1 at London Bridge appears to be taking some interest in Dick's presence with a camera while a Charing Cross–Sevenoaks working draws into platform 2. It was to the left of the island platform 3 and 4 that the London & Croydon Railway, despite arriving on the south side of the Greenwich Railway's formation, built a terminus to the north of the L&GR for its opening on 5th June 1839. The folly of the two companies' trains having to cross one another was soon appreciated, and exacerbated when traffic increased with the arrival of the Brighton in August 1841 and the South Eastern a year later. Agreement to swap stations was reached as early as 1840; the Greenwich, then widening the approach viaduct, completed it in 1842. But it was another two years before the exchange took place. By all accounts the Croydon got the raw end of the deal because the Greenwich terminus was a rather crude affair. Worse still perhaps, the Greenwich refused to make any contribution toward the cost of improvement. The former Croydon terminus was swept away during construction of The Charing Cross Railway, authorised in 1859. Much of the cost was the result of some rather underhand, perhaps even unethical, moves by the powerful and influential Trustees of St Thomas's Hospital. About one-sixth of an acre of their grounds was required for the line and though the buildings were untouched they managed to have a clause inserted in the Bill stating they could later call on the railway to purchase all of the grounds. Inevitably they did, demanding £750,000, nearly 90% of the CCR's capital, cut to £296,000 on arbitration. The present St Thomas's Hospital, opposite Westminster, was built with that railway money. The Charing Cross Railway opened on 11th January 1864, the branch into Cannon Street on 1st September 1866. One other point to note, and something not seen nowadays, is the porter pushing one of those heavy trolleys along the platform. Has he perhaps just loaded parcels or luggage into the front Guards van of the Gravesend train? *RCR 10327*

Opposite top: The Dulwich College Estates were influential enough to keep railways off their land but could not prevent the construction of lines along the borders. But they did manage to ensure bridges on those lines were less of a blot on the landscape by having clauses placed in the contracts stating these had to be decorative. This one is over London Road in Forest Hill though the road becomes Lordship Lane on the other side of the bridge and that was the name given to the adjacent station. The photograph was taken on 3rd March 1957, 2½ years after the line to Crystal Palace (High Level) closed. Was the distant signal still mounted in hope the line remained dormant rather than dead? *RCR 8118A*

11 Odds and Ends

Middle: Photographs of freight trains crossing the Deptford Lift Bridge are by no means uncommon but those of the other form of transport using it are rare. On 2nd June 1958 Richard was on hand to photograph the lighter 'Trout' *en route* to the Surrey Commercial Docks being drawn under the lifted section by a motor barge. The Brighton Line viaduct forms a backdrop. *RCR 12538*

Bottom: There could not be many coal offices as splendid and grand as the one occupied by Messrs H Cooper & Co., but then it is attached to the Victorian building provided to serve visitors to the Crystal Palace. The station opened on 1st August 1865 with the branch from Nunhead but closed in January 1917 as an economy measure. Reopening in March 1919 it closed again in May 1944 to reopen for the last time in 1946. By that time usage of the branch had reached a low point, especially as the Crystal Palace had burned down in 1936 to deprive the line of its *raison d-etre.* Moreover the near parallel Brighton line but ¾-mile or so to the east between Brockley and Sydenham offered a more attractive service. The low traffic level, once estimated as an average of five passengers per train at the terminus, could not justify the expense of renewing the power cabling. The branch closed on 20th September 1954, a month before Dick took this photograph, though this once magnificent terminus was not demolished until 1961. After years of neglect the vaulted brick subway below Crystal Palace Parade that permitted visitors to pass between station and palace dry shod was renovated and is now Grade II* listed and occasionally open to the public. *RCR 5575*

Above: Mercers Crossing Signals photographed on 13th November 1954, a pleasant, quiet South Eastern box in pleasant outer suburban surroundings perhaps? Er, no. To the left of it the ranks of sidings and constantly busy happenings of Bricklayers Arms goods depot lead on to the dusty, smoke-laden sheds and repair shop of 73B, Bricklayers Arms loco depot. To the right is the multiplicity of marshalling and goods sidings under the guardianship of the big North Kent West Junction box. Maybe Mercers Crossing cannot compare but it was obviously important enough to have the locking room windows bricked up to minimise interior damage should it be targeted during the war. 73B closed in 1962 but the goods depot lasted until 1981: the signal box had been decommissioned some years earlier. *RCR 5638*

Right: Dick was at Herne Hill on 4th November 1961 to witness the last two of the splendid Wainwright/ Maunsell 4-4-0s, 'D1' No 31749 and 'E1' No 31067, come up the rise from Brixton as they head to Ashford for breaking up. I wonder if this was one of the 'tip-offs'' he occasionally received, for this is most definitely THE END. What more is there to add?